What People Are Saying About *Am I Bad?*

"*AM I BAD?* is a *tour de force* of the tortured landscape of child abuse and its pernicious long-term outcomes. Numerous case studies expertly intertwine with theoretical insights to produce the equivalent of a comprehensive and unconventional treatment modality. This book is an important contribution towards the edification of victims and institutions alike."

—Sam Vaknin, PhD, author *Malignant Self-Love*

"You bring out some very enlightening experiences that certainly back up your theories. Having worked in both a county mental-health clinic and an 800-bed mental health facility, I found your compassion and unique style of therapy refreshing."

—Pam English, mental health professional

"I will recommend your book to everyone on our mailing list. I would agree that child abuse has a major influence on the development of one's personality... living in an abusive environment tends to [make a child] unable to explore or discover his or her own self."

—Cindy, Cornell University

"This is a wonderful book. It should be compulsory reading for anyone dealing with abused children or abused adults, or adult survivors of childhood abuse: physicians, psychologists and other therapists, teachers, protective workers and so on. And the language is so clear and non-technical that it will be of enormous benefit to the survivors of trauma themselves, and even to parents who want to ensure the safety and wellbeing of their children."
—Robert Rich, PhD

"Your materials (testing for child/domestic abuse) are great! I really hate child/domestic abuse because it is also practiced by many tribes here in Tanzania."

—Filemoni Tenu, Muhimbili University, Tanzania

"I have found that almost two thirds of the women that I have interviewed present a long history of abuse as the main etiology of their depression. I will translate your tests and use them in my practice."
—Ricardo Villamizar, Clinical Psychologist,
Marin General Hospital, Ecuador

"For many years as an independent midwife, I had the opportunity to identify and acknowledge women's past and current experience of abuse. Pregnancy is a 'raw' open time when many memories, feelings surface, whether the woman wants them to or not. I have personally observed that it is an opportunity to begin/ continue a healing process."
—Jill Demilew, Kings Healthcare Trust, London

"I am currently working on a USAID-funded Women's Health and Family Welfare Project in Indonesia. We are very interested in using your tests on child abuse and domestic violence and will translate them."
—Harriet Beazley, Ph.D.,
Women's Health & Family Welfare Project, Indonesia

"It is, indeed, kind of you to make available your inventories for measuring domestic violence against both women and children. I am a Health Social Scientist from India and will conduct some reliability studies here."
—Hemant Kulkami, M.D.

"I have frequent contact with both elementary school age children and with unwed mothers, many of whom I suspect were sexually abused as children. I am sure your work will be helpful."
—Barbara Franks-Morra, R.N, M.F.A.

AM I BAD ?

Recovering from Abuse

HEYWARD BRUCE EWART, III, PH.D.

New Horizons in Therapy Series

Library of Congress Cataloging-in-Publication Data

Ewart, Heyward Bruce, 1943-
  Am I bad ? : recovering from abuse / Heyward Bruce Ewart III. -- 1st ed.
       p. cm. -- (New horizons in therapy series ; bk. #6)
  Includes bibliographical references (p.   ) and index.
  ISBN-13: 978-1-932690-33-0 (pbk. : alk. paper)
  ISBN-10: 1-932690-33-6 (pbk. : alk. paper)
  1. Child abuse--United States--Case studies. 2. Family violence--United States--Case studies. I. Title.
  HV6626.52.E94 2007
  362.76--dc22
                                        2007010591

Distributed by:
Baker & Taylor, Ingram Book Group, New Leaf Distributing

Published by:
Loving Healing Press
5145 Pontiac Trail
Ann Arbor, MI 48105
USA

http://www.LovingHealing.com or
info@LovingHealing.com
Fax +1 734 663 6861

Loving Healing Press

Loving Healing Press

The New Horizons in Therapy Series

- Got parts? An Insider's Guide to Managing Life Successfully with Dissociative Identity Disorder

- Coping with Physical Loss and Disability: A Workbook

- Why Good People Make Bad Choices: How You Can Develop Peace Of Mind Through Integrity,

- Regaining Control: When Love Becomes A Prison

- Am I Bad? Recovering from Abuse

About our Series Editor, Robert Rich, Ph.D.

Robert Rich, M.Sc., Ph.D., M.A.P.S., A.A.S.H. is a highly experienced counseling psychologist. His web site www.anxietyanddepression-help.com is a storehouse of helpful information for people suffering from anxiety and depression.

Bob is also a multiple award-winning writer of both fiction and non-fiction, and a professional editor. His writing is displayed at www.bobswriting.com. You are advised not to visit him there unless you have the time to get lost for a while.

Three of his books are tools for psychological self-help: *Anger and Anxiety, Personally Speaking,* and *Cancer: A personal challenge.* Dr. Rich currently resides at Wombat Hollow in Australia.

Contents

Psychometric Instruments

To: Mom, Caroline M. Ewart,

who left this life July 2, 2006.

and to my children: Melissa, Stephanie, Kristen,

Jennifer, Alexandra, and Rebecca

Foreword

Somewhere in the world today sits a woman in a hospital emergency room with her head hung low; body posture in a slumped, negative position; she is probably bleeding from an uncommon place on her body; a rape kit is being prepared by the nursing staff and a criminal offense report is being filled out by a police officer. From this description you already know this woman has been sexually assaulted.

What the description doesn't tell you is the mindset of this woman. Being a former police officer, my experience, after countless numbers of these types of instances, is that this victim's mindset is "This is my fault." No matter the age, education, background or circumstance, when the police report is written and the questioning begins, the victim will blame herself for being assaulted.

In his book: *AM I BAD? Recovering from Abuse* Dr. Heyward Ewart brilliantly brings this type of thinking to light, stating "Every child blames herself for the abuse or neglect she has suffered. The message, deeply internalized, navigates the individual throughout life." Experience also tells me that this is not the first time she has suffered this type of abuse, at the hands of what I like to call a "domestic terrorist".

Domestic in relationship, known or unknown to the victim, this type of terrorist is not hiding in caves, carrying grenade launchers down city streets or flying planes into buildings; no, this terrorist is convincing the innocence in a child or the grace in a woman that she is to blame for being abused, thereby holding the child or the woman hostage in her own mind!

This type of mindset ultimately leads the victim to self-destructive behaviors, not the commonplace self-destruction that we see daily, but the kind that puts limitations in the mind of the victim. The result leaves her mentally seeking relationships with those who would be abusers. Dr. Ewart, being right on point, makes this perfectly clear when he states, "The abused little girl becomes the abused adolescent, who becomes an abused adult. Just as water seeks its own level, so an abused person seeks relationships and a lifestyle that are no better than what she believes she deserves."

Am I Bad? Recovering from Abuse is masterfully written, with questions, answers, case studies and strong, clear facts. This book should not just sit on the bookshelves of psychologists and counselors. It should be open on the desk and readily available to draw from its wealth of knowledge that the author has penned, not just for us in the field but for everyone who will ever come in contact with those who have been abused and need to understand that *it is not your fault!!*

Rev. Lawrence Stevenson, Founder/CEO
National Agenda
www.nationalagenda.net
Author, *From the Inside out: A Look Into Teen Violence and Rebellion.*

Introduction

Child abuse and domestic violence are a dual pandemic. They are often linked, for the first can lead to the second, in my experience. Many professionals are surprised at this observation, but I have attempted to show the connection in this volume. An abused child becomes prone to abuse in adulthood. Although both subjects have been extensively studied, much of the literature deals only with a description of each. Rarely are they discussed together. Moreover, existing documentation tends only to describe in general how horrible child abuse is, both in degree and in frequency, and how hopeless the struggle of society is to stop domestic violence from continuing to skyrocket. Stopping domestic violence altogether has received little scholarly attention.

The literature is thus replete with accounts of what is happening in our culture, but little has been written about why. One of the most important factors in domestic violence has been overlooked in research and in practice; that is, the treatment of the affliction. Too often, shelters provide a haven for a time, but when the victim is released, she either returns to the same abuser or seeks out a worse one. Not only is the cycle not broken, but the victim becomes even more vulnerable.

The purpose of this book is not to provide treatment techniques, although some principles are mentioned, but to furnish from real-life case histories a penetrating and hopefully unforgettable look at what causes domestic violence: child abuse. Vivid understanding of the cause must precede the development of effective treatment. Further, the intent is to show many other consequences of child abuse, most importantly a distorted sense of self, which greatly limits the chances of a fulfilling life. Child abuse implants false messages about who one is. It is most difficult to live a successful life that is based on lies.

When clinicians and others with the power to produce change really see what child abuse does, the adult ramifi-

cations of this phenomenon can be treated with permanent success.

1 Disintegration of Life

Pretty little Amy, only nine years old, was playing near her inner-city home when a stranger raped her in full view of her young friends. Worse than the assault was her father's condemnation that placed full blame on her for letting it happen, and the onset of rejection. His words, "It's your own fault," formed an unceremonious branding of the child as a "less-than" that would be confirmed by periodic acts of sexual assaults against her as time went on. Each subsequent violation of her personhood was committed by people who were supposed to love her, not by strangers.

By the time she entered her teen years, the original Amy was gone. There remained the form of a maturing female who knew no power of her own except for the ability to gain attention and meet survival needs through the sexual use of her body. So she sold it in order to exist. When she discovered that crack cocaine worked miraculously to lift her away from the anguish of nonexistence, she became a loyal slave to it.

She was only in her late teens when her body would no longer bring enough money for both living and crack. So she sold her body for crack only. She came down with pneumonia, and while in the hospital she was diagnosed with AIDS. It was found that that she had carried the virus for a very long time. She estimated that she might have infected more than 150 men. Even while she was hospitalized, with oxygen at her nose and, a feeding tube in her throat, and intravenous lines in her veins, she continued to accept the clients who came to her hospital room for their usual service. She lived almost two years after the first hospitalization, but because her lifestyle remained unchanged, she was dead by 24.

Larry – Growing up Abused

Larry was neglected in foster homes from birth to age 2, when the real trouble began. His adoptive father hated him. He was yelled at, beaten, thrown out to agencies, brought back, cursed, ignored, insulted, and belittled until he was farmed out permanently to a boys' home in his early teens. His adoptive mother, living in terror that her husband might kill both of them, kept her mouth shut and even remained living with the man long after the boy had grown up.

To this day, the young man has told no-one but his therapist that when he was four he used to wake up from nightmares about something hard and slimy under his blanket. When he awoke and felt the mattress, he wondered where the substance came from and what it was.

All of his life, he was tormented by his uncertain sexual identity. Even as this book was being written, he wondered whether he was bi-sexual or homosexual. But there is one thing he knows for sure: He is gay, and in his mind, it's his rightful punishment.

Love of money has been called the root of all kinds of evil. But child abuse is a root that runs deeper, spreads farther, and holds a specific, predictable consequence: the loss of personhood and often of life itself.

While AIDS is only one example, it is a recurring demonstration of abuse leading to a deadly disease. When a mind is set off course, the body follows.

In 2004, I presented a continuing education class on domestic violence for a medical center in Jacksonville, Florida. I began my remarks with this statement "Domestic violence begins at age four." Abuse at the hands of a partner in early adulthood does not arise out of a vacuum merely by the poor choice of a mate. Rather, maltreatment from this stage on is very often the natural outcome of a type of "brainwashing" that begins early and receives reinforcement many times through the years.

It is during the early years that humans acquire their first ideas about who they are, and, unfortunately, they believe these falsehoods for the rest of their lives. Victims are initiated into a pattern of abuse, including self abuse, not in adulthood, but in childhood. As a matter of fact, every one of us comes into adulthood with a second-hand opinion of who we are.

When a little child is called brilliant, stupid, beautiful, ugly, hopeless, helpless, good, bad, a blessing or a curse, the child has no choice but to accept these assertions as "gospel". What other source of information does he have? He can absorb only the information available to him.

These messages are communicated just as well or better by what is unsaid. The glances, the pauses, the scowls, the smiles, the visual forces, speak indelibly, although without sound. The child's self-definition derives from these impressions. They are permanent; like initials carved in the bark of a young tree that only enlarge as the tree grows.

You may have wondered by now why an example of male abuse has been included in our opening case histories, when little girls are abused, especially sexually, far more often. The reason is that the effects are the same. Female sexual abuse is far more prevalent. A press release by the U.S. Department of Health and Human Services (1996), revealed that girls are sexually abused three times more often than boys but that boys have a greater risk of emotional neglect and serious injury. According to the same source, abuse and neglect cases rose from 1.4 million in 1986 to nearly 3 million in 1993. The number of seriously injured nearly quadrupled from 143 thousand to 570 thousand in the same time period. I am using the pronoun "he" only as common practice in describing child development.

When the child reaches adolescence, having mastered the lessons about who he is, he is driven to experiment. His concept of self may not work in the peer group, so various trial personalities and their accompanying behavior must be rotated until one works. Not to fit in means annihilation, not just rejection, and today the consequences can mean physical attacks as well. Clothes with the wrong label might literally be torn from his back.

In adulthood, the urgency to meet life on its own terms; that is, deal with the challenges of living, becomes more pressing, with countless choices to be made. One's identity, or a solid sense of who one is, determines the direction of these choices. But this idea of "self" is no more than a chance configuration. It is formed by combining the second-hand opinions received in childhood with the results of adolescent experimentation. Victims enter adult life with the greatest possible handicap: believing they know who they are and being wrong, or, alternatively, having no idea whatsoever. Either case requires dependence on someone else.

While child abuse might harshly be stated as "raping the personality", even children reared in fairly normal homes still suffer a "molestation" of their identity through the communication of false information about themselves. The messages can even be seemingly positive. I have met nearly-retarded people who were told all of their lives that they were brilliant, and the result was a life of endless frustration as they attempted to achieve goals that were impossible for them. And worse, they left unattended very great possibilities in other realms that would have paid off with great enrichment.

But the tragedies I have seen over 20 years of practice mostly result from destructive, even malicious, assertions about the child's nature on the part of parents, teachers, siblings, and other influential members of the early social circle. This "programming" has cheated them out of a fulfilling life that could have fostered the greatest joy of all: being and celebrating their own self. Indeed, for those who are spiritual, blossoming into the fullness of one's being, with the hidden talents, gifts, and abilities thoroughly explored, is the highest honor to one's Creator, however that divine entity may be defined. It might even be argued that such is the highest form of praise. One victim proclaimed:

For the first time in my life, I have been given the greatest sense of freedom: to know that the career I have chosen, that of a dedicated mother and wife, reflects the real 'me' and therefore is honorable, is a huge joy. I don't have to listen to the old messages, that I'm no good, that I'm bad.

I have spent my whole life feeling like a worthless piece of sh—. No matter how hard I tried, my father and step-mother would always put me down. I could do nothing to make them happy, to accept me. I could not make them give me the affection and feeling of worth I need so badly.

I'm not to blame for their inabilities as parents. I'm learning that I didn't cause their unhappiness, that the messages I was given as a child were false.

I have always believed bad things happened because I was a bad girl, that I was unworthy to have a mother, that it was my fault that a neighbor molested me—my fault because I was the one who went into his house.

I have let people abuse me verbally and physically because I believed that is what I deserved. Today, I'm learning I don't deserve to be treated that way. I am finding myself, my true self!

There is hope for people like me, and I believe if doctors become aware of what child abuse does, people like me can recover instead of being misdiagnosed, institutionalized, given improper medications, and ending up suicidal.

The Statistical Evidence

As far back as 1997, 41 states reported that nearly 1,000 children were known by child protective agencies to have died as a result of abuse or neglect in each state reporting. These agencies further estimated reports of physical abuse at the 3-million mark nationwide, but admit that a high but unknown percentage of cases are never reported. (U.S. Dept. Health and Human Services, 1997).

Recent statistics are even more staggering, as illustrated by one single state, South Carolina. The website Childwelfare.com, hosted by Duncan Lindsey, indicates a child population of 1,009,641, with 11,246 of these children abused in 2002 alone. (This is a national site, where your own state can be examined.) Nationally, this source reports the highest percentage of abuse to occur in the 0 to 3 age group (16%), followed by 4 to 7 (13.7 %), then, 8 to 11 (11.9%), 12 to 15 (10.6%), and 16 to 17 (6.0%).

But as serious as these abuses are, they do not match the greatest damage: the message that abuse implants in the child permanently.

Another patient reports:

> I used to have images cross my mind, then quickly dismiss them. I had no reason to believe anything like sexual abuse had happened to me. After all, no-one in my family had said anything tragic had happened to me or my family when I was four years old.
>
> My pain escalated in adulthood until I was brave enough to consider that something had happened and gave myself permission to explore the idea. I was like a computer unable to proceed until the sequence was right. I've learned to pay attention to these images—that is, flashbacks— sometimes visual, sometimes almost being audible, all packed with feelings.
>
> My molestation was filled with emotional messages which I have believed for 43 years. My assailant was my "true love". "Don't tell anyone. They won't like you," he said. These messages were recalled only by my being in a group. While others were sharing, little pieces of my own life started to come together.
>
> It has been a lot of painstaking emotional pain to discover all this, but it's been worth it, to

be able to proceed with my life. Now, at 43, I am finally rid of the garbage and reasonably happy.

When my molester almost got caught, he abandoned me, and left me feeling false guilt, that it was my fault. To make matters worse, I was a victim of a dysfunctional, negative, and abusive family that fed on my weakness. I was the oldest of seven children and was told how to feel, how not to feel, so I believed I had no right to my own feelings. That apparently made it harder to discover what I do feel and to trust those feelings as cues to my recovery. I couldn't do anything fast enough or well enough to meet their approval, adding to my distress.

The weather even had an affect on me. The sun casting a certain shadow triggered deep emotional feelings of fear, sadness, and aloneness. The same with certain sounds and music. I am learning to pay attention to these things, to recognize them and deal with them and get healthy.

Too few professionals are up to date on what they need to know about the devastation of child abuse. The American Professional Society on the Abuse of Children (APSAC), an organization I highly value and depend upon. conducted a survey of professional needs (APSAC, 1994).

There is simply not enough competent help for abuse victims. Interdisciplinary people working in the field cited as the most difficult aspects of their work, "heavy workload, low pay, public laws and policies that impede my work, and lack of communication with interdisciplinary colleagues."

One woman believes she would not have survived if she had not found our therapy group. A psychiatric nurse as well as a survivor of child and domestic abuse, she says our understanding and treatment go far beyond what is now being offered in the field at large.

They have given me an understanding of the trauma, so that I can live with it, on a daily basis. Healing of trauma takes time, understanding, encouragement, and compassion that few professionals are willing or able to give, in my experience. My doctor has been gifted in this field. He has saved my life and given me a sense of peace within that I have searched for in a therapist for years. The ideas he presents make sense and give people hope that they can overcome the trauma that has been inflicted on them.

APSAC reports that child protective agencies nationally were able to investigate only 28 percent of cases in which children were harmed by maltreatment in 1993, compared with 44 percent in 1986. An anonymous, inner-city teacher, writing in the Society's booklet, "Connecting with Kids," reports,

I see a lot of this kind of thing [child abuse], but D was one of the most troubling kids I'd seen. At seven years of age, he was fatalistic, foul-mouthed, and jumpy. He was hypervigilant—he seemed scared all the time, and he was utterly unable to concentrate. You'd see a flash of sweetness in him now and then, but mostly he was too on-guard for that.

The day he came in with a welt on his cheek, I decided it was time to call child protective services. The caseworker hooked up with the police to do a home visit, where they found total chaos—filth, rotating boyfriends, violence among the adults, violence in the neighborhood. Both the mom and several of her boyfriends had been in and out of prison. Mom had dealt some drugs. Years ago, people would have said that D was a "troublemaker"—now we say he's a kid suffering from post-traumatic stress disorder as a result of violence in his home and neighborhood. (APSAC Advisor).

Post-traumatic stress disorder (PTSD)is one of the more easily definable outcomes of child abuse. Most severely victimized children, in my experience, can be accurately diagnosed for PTSD. Not until adulthood, when life stresses compound, do they eventually seek treatment; that is, those few who do. As for the children, they are often diagnosed with hyperactivity, attention-deficit disorder.

Traumatized people often abuse alcohol and other drugs. They are found everywhere at Alcoholics Anonymous and Narcotics Anonymous meetings. Current estimates of the number of female incest survivors in A.A. range from 40 to 80 percent. Similarly, about an equal percentage of men in these groups have survived some sort of physical abuse as children, according to many studies. (A.A. World Services, New York 1998). Nearly 100 percent of these victims have never been treated. Those who relapse the most—or completely give up—tend to be those who have been through the worst nightmares that life has to offer children.

The public at large seems to blame the male homosexual for the AIDS epidemic. However, the group spreading the disease most rapidly today consists of intravenous drug abusers. Many of them, perhaps easily the majority, were pointed toward the needle not by the peer group but by the abuse in childhood. Perhaps some make it all the way to elementary school before their true selves are mangled. But one thing is sure in my experience: Rarely does a substance abuser know who he is.

<table>
<tr><td>2</td><td><h1>Recovering of Self</h1></td><td></td></tr>
</table>

A New Developmental Model

The average reader is likely familiar with the established models of personality development. For example, one school, espoused by Rothbart (1988) and Kagan (Kaplan, 1993, 1989) link inborn temperament to adjustment in later life. Freud sees development as progressing through a series of psychosexual stages (FreudNet, 1996). Erickson (Ames, 1993) was the first to stress social factors in personality formation, and he emphasized such concepts as trust versus mistrust and identity versus role confusion.

Levinson (1986) divided the lifespan into transitional stages and introduced the concept of "midlife crisis". Baumrind (1991) saw styles of parenting as being factors in personality formation.

It can readily be seen that the more recent theorists progress toward a realization of interpersonal events as major factors directing the course of maturation from infancy to adulthood. They are getting closer to the truth. I, however, take a much different approach. Instead of describing how children might ideally develop, I propose a model based on what I have seen as a clinician, treating most known forms of emotional distress and crippling mental disorders for 25 years. My premise is that all children, to some degree, absorb erroneous information about themselves that can misdirect their course through life, prevent full maturation no matter what model is used to measure, and create a false identity. I have named this the "adopted self". This adopted self can work rather successfully when a child has been fortunate in his life experiences, although it is not the "real self". Children who are "lied to" about their nature are destined to acquire an adopted self that limits life in direct proportion to the severity of the false information. Child abuse is the worst case, where the most severe lies are communicated most often and most forcefully.

As mentioned briefly in Chapter 1, all people cross the line from childhood to adulthood with a secondhand opinion of who they are. Without any questioning, we take as truth whatever our parents and other influentials have said about us during our formative years, whether these message are communicated verbally, physically, or silently.

Children have two basic vulnerabilities that directly pertain to this model. One, they are gullible and two, their sources of information are limited. They must depend on whatever information is available to form a concept of self.

Similarly, even parents who are capable and who would be considered loving, are not perfect. Thus, even the best-intentioned parent cannot, without a flaw, consistently convey the truth about a child to that child.

These impressions, accumulated by the child, then later combined with an idea of what the world will accept, form most of the construct of self image. No matter how absurdly false, these early impressions are the ones that register deeply and permanently, and that we automatically accept as true to a very large extent. Even those experiences we vividly remember, wherein we rejected an accusation or railed against some falsehood asserted against us, have their penetrating and lasting impact because we do not totally disbelieve them.

The adopted self is the personal image we use to operate in adult life. It should be self-evident to all that there is a "true self" that exists somewhere, that we were born with, and that forms the substance of who we are in fact. There must be some way that this true self can be accessed. It can be, and that method is discussed later in the chapter on treatment considerations. But let it be said right here that the discovery of the true self is the successful outcome of therapy for many of the most common psychological disorders. This is the "pearl of great price," whose uncovering should be the goal in the treatment of many conditions.

In common with other models of development, the adopted self progresses through a series of stages. These milestones are measured in terms of power acquisition, experimentation, and ingesting the impressions formed during these processes. Of great importance is the internal impact of information communicated about one's self through the process.

I postulate (see Table 2-1 on p. 14) that the true self, which many religions regard as the "soul," is fully expressed from before birth to about age 2. But abuse and neglect can stifle this freedom. At age two, the child is able to attach significant meaning to the messages of others. Also, in this age period, there is no sense of power but only of freedom to act.

From age 2 to 6, the self is modified, but not substantially changed, by required and forbidden behaviors that have consequences determined by the caregiver. During this stage, there is imaged power, and in fact the imagination plays a major role in self determination. The greater the imagination, the greater the range of choices for thought material later in life.

By age 6, and continuing up to the edge of adolescence, the self becomes subordinated to both opinion and experience. It is in this period that claims or comments are made by others as to the character, worth, and abilities of the child, which the child internalizes.

Of course, the interaction with parents or parental surrogates has the greatest influence. When a father or mother is especially forceful, or in some way very effective, in what is said about the child, the impression is more difficult to remove—as if the information becomes encapsulated or "wired into" the developing brain, forever protected and able to become more influential, not less, as time passes. This "capsule" is more active in adulthood than in childhood. A great-grandmother will recite her capsule as readily as a newly-wed.

	Womb to 2	**Age 2-6**	**Age 6-13**	**Adoles- cence**
Development of adopted self	True self dominates	Self molded	Self altered	Trial selves rotate
Power	No power	Imaginary power	Pretended power	Struggle for power
Freedom	No free- dom	Loss of freedom	Pretended Freedom	Struggle for freedom
Messages	Receptive to	Resisted	Receptive again	Struggle to reject

Table 2-1: Formation of the Adopted Self

Also in this stage (age 6-13), there is "pretended power," as opposed to imaginary power. Here is when you see young boys tying towels around their shoulders and jumping out of trees as though they could fly like superman. In addition, severely maltreated children will form ideas of their revenge, which they increasingly are carry out.

Even conscientious, loving parents fail to examine the accuracy or timing of the messages they give. Besides what is said outright, parents and other intimates communicate just as deeply by what they do not say—even by facial expressions by which a father may strike terror in the heart of his young son or daughter. Day after day, the identity is being formed, malformed or misformed. Abuse or neglect at this stage, as we shall see later, often mangles any truth the child may have obtained about himself.

Good parents, without knowing, have their own agenda, at least sometimes, when they make remarks about the child. Such exclamations as "You're just like your father," for example, can say nothing about the child but everything about the parent. In addressing their children, parents vent their own misconceptions, hopes, fears, confusion, and doubts. They unknowingly describe their own identity when they try to describe their child.

This is an appropriate place to point out a very great tragedy, which grown sons and daughters increasingly must accept at some stage. While virtually all children love their parents unconditionally, not all parents love their children.

When a child is maliciously denied access to his real personhood, he is doomed to spend his life in a trial-and-error process of discovery in which every piece of evidence is questionable. This choice, and the acceptance of the lies as true, are the only alternatives.

Again referring to Table 2-1 (p. 14), the adolescent carries but a remnant of the true self of infancy. He may believe his accumulation of messages or he may reject them, but he is not certain either way. He doesn't know who he is or who he wants to be. Besides this fact, acceptance by the peer group becomes paramount. At the very time when the child most needs his parents, he will have nothing to do with their beliefs and will sever himself from family ties to some extent—often as completely as possible.

The adolescent must somehow gather the strength to experiment with various trial "personalities" in order to find one that is suitable for the peer group. A maltreated child will not be up to this enormously challenging task and will develop symptoms. He will drop out. He will get into rebellion, very often including drug or alcohol abuse. Others, not as badly treated, will give the process a try but not succeed. They fail to find a combination that works, and thus they are rejected by the group. Such an outcome introduces a "less-than" mentality with which to enter adulthood.

Survival Needs

A critically important factor added to this new developmental model is the concept of survival needs.

It is my assertion that the needs of the child are the needs of the adult. That is, needs do not change, and they do not go away. Even when needs are met, they remain to be fulfilled again and again. When not met, they will scream out in the form of behavioral, affective, cognitive, or personality disorders either episodically or chronically. The most important need in the maturation process at any stage is affirmation of the true self.

Several of the extant models, such as those of Piaget and Erickson, emphasize needs in childhood. But the reason that needs are permanent throughout life is that they arise from the true self, from the child within us all. The adopted self of adulthood is not the real person but only an artificial construct. The true self is the one who comes directly from the womb.

Correct verbal and nonverbal messages on the part of parents is always crucial, even in adolescence. A boy needs a father, and a girl needs a mother, just as much as in earlier stages. A father who has suffered neglect or rejection by his own father will not only be hampered but often utterly crippled in his ability to be open, approachable and affectionate, especially to a son.

The effect of an inadequate father, whether neglectful or demanding, is never less than devastating to the son's personhood. The son is prevented from having a full sense of being a male. Father is the one who grants the "right of passage" to manhood, and he is also the one who can block it. If the boy sees no hand extended and hears no voice saying in some way, "Welcome to manhood," he never fully "arrives" in his own mind but carries the sense of being more boy than man all his life.

A daughter denied affirmation by a father lives out her whole life with a sense of not completely existing. The lives of such unfortunates are continuous efforts to stave off the fear of annihilation—worse than the fear of death. Feeling as though one doesn't exist is more terrifying than the knowledge that one will some day die.

Daughters go to extremes to counteract this bottomless deficit. They will take a tyrannical father and make him in their own fantasies a sweet, wonderful man. Or they will search for their "real father" in relationship after relationship, never realizing whom they are really leaving each time they break from a partner. They will fight their own buried conviction that they must indeed be loathsome if "My own father couldn't love me," and they will invariably transfer these voids and fears onto their concept of God.

Sometimes they will sell their bodies with the meager comfort of feeling that "I must be worth something if men will pay money for me." A similar phenomenon can be seen in the ambitious model or actress who endlessly pursues some important person to "take my picture." The personal account of one of my own recent patients graphically illustrates the point:

> I married at 17, was a virgin, and wanted to leave home. I rationalized a lot, you see. I prided myself in the fact that I stayed a virgin, although my parents were very strict. I married the first man I dated. I got pregnant on my honeymoon.
>
> When my husband later beat me and my 3-month-old daughter, I divorced him. My dad moved me and my daughter back home. The second man I had sex with looked surprised when I asked him if he was going to hurt me, and he said, "No." What I meant to ask was whether he was going to hurt me emotionally, and he did. All I meant to him was sex.
>
> The one thing I was proud of, being a virgin, was long gone. So I rationalized that this was the cause of my increasing promiscuity. I was good at rationalizing. I made up my own philosophies, and then would change them or add to them to make some sense of the deep emotional wounds with a tremendous amount of pain. My parents were too strict. I regretted ever being such a good girl. Why didn't I go ahead and just have sex before marriage? After all, I probably wouldn't have ended up beaten and I wouldn't have had the silly dreams that I could actually be happily married or just plain old happy. It wasn't until recently that I found out that I was set up for all of this from the age of 4.
>
> My mom was physically and verbally abused when she was growing up, and her dad was alcoholic. My dad was an alcoholic from a divorced

home, and both of his parents were killed by automobiles when my dad was very young, around 11 or 12. He lived with his mom's parents after his mom and dad divorced when he was about 7. His mom moved 300 miles away to find work and didn't see him often, but made sure he was well dressed.

Dad had a sister who was diagnosed as schizophrenic in her 40s, after she cursed out the phone company and served time in prison for it. That's almost all I know about my parents' histories. Dad doesn't talk much about his family. He is a very emotional man but emotionally unavailable to me.

That brings me to the remembrance of one of the many times he hurt my feelings and one of my brothers came out to comfort me. He told me I had to understand my dad was a drill sergeant and a military policeman in the Army. His way of treating me was to make me tough. I didn't buy it then, and I still don't buy it now; nor do I excuse it. This thing runs in families, you know. This is a dysfunction, if you haven't guessed yet.

There was a lot of verbal and physical abuse from my parents. But no matter how bad it was, my mother's reply was that our life was never as bad as what she had to endure growing up. "I did the best I could, and I treated all you kids the same," she would say. "I don't think I did too bad when I was raising you kids, and I wouldn't have anyone but your dad. He's the only man for me." All this when I know different.

My dad's responses, behavior, and attitude were always—and I mean always—negative. Except, of course, when it came to babies. He had seven of us, and he could handle babies. He loved babies. But when each of us became about 5 years old, the distance began. I know. I watched it happen.

I was the oldest of us seven. It was, most of the time, "It's too hot" or "It's too cold." "You're stupid." "That's stupid." "What's wrong with you?" "Your hair looks like sh—." "You should know better." "You always have your head up your a--." Etc., etc., and then... total indifference.

It was, and still is, impossible to get any warmth from him, and I really tried all my life. About one and half years ago, I really thought I had caught on to something when, at the funeral of my 19-year-old nephew, I was really hurting from seeing him in the casket for the first time, and I held onto my daddy and asked him to tell me he loved me. And he did, and even patted me gently on the back and gave me a hug.

The first time I called to chat after that, I ended the conversation with "I love you." And he said, "I love you." I really thought things had changed. I was so happy. The next time I called I ended with "I love you," and the response was, "yeah."

In late adolescence, the young person begins for the first time to consider the future and begins to look at various occupations. The choice of the way to make a living is restricted to "no more than I deserve," just as the choice of a partner is limited by the same measure.

Many daughters are brought up with the unspoken message that their job for life is to serve Mother. A mother companion can be guaranteed success by convincing the daughter from the earliest time that there is something not quite right about her (the child) and that she can never make it on her own.

Mothers who place little value on their daughters' lives compared to their own can have a servant for life by always being unhappy and never letting the daughter please her fully. There was once in my care a 67-year-old woman who 40 years previously had divorced her husband in favor of coming back to Mother. Mother, now 93, was still not pleased at all with her daughter, who complained during one session, "Dr. Ewart, my mother treats me like a little girl. I'm not a little girl. I'm a big girl." Then Mother shot back, "Then act like one!"

This daughter was a retired director of nursing at a major medical center. In her professional career, she enjoyed the highest respect and recognition of her colleagues. But none of them had designs on her as a servant.

The same tragic "game" can play between a mother and her son. Never having gotten her needs met through her husband, she turns to her son for emotional support. Some young men—and some not so young—find that drug or alcohol abuse provides justification for never leaving home. It is more face-saving to be home due to addictive disease than to be there because you can't leave your mother.

Some men go to another extreme: having an extramarital affair in order to destroy the marriage, after which they can go home. Such men have then been able to say that the marriage was destroyed by an affair rather than the primary need to go home. The same happens with women. In fact, one of the main causes of infidelity in my experience is the need to go back home. Often I can quickly determine the cause of the breakup by watching where the partners go once the marriage is over. Husband and wives have been shocked to discover in therapy that it wasn't a sexual tryst that did them in but in fact an emotional affair with a parent.

Having come through the emotion-charged personality experiments of adolescence, the adult's sense of identity is now an adopted self, a culmination of earlier opinions plus the trial and error of the teens. It is this adopted self that governs the adult, with the result that very few individuals ever take a look back and question the messages of childhood. Most people go to their graves without an accurate idea of who they are or who they should have become.

The Sense of Becoming

The "sense of becoming" is related to the perception of power discussed earlier. A sense of "being" and of having power are required in order to stave off the fear of annihilation, the greatest of all fears that mankind retains. A sense of becoming fosters the substance of being, and with being comes power. The greater the sense of being, the greater the sense of power to resist the fear of annihilation, that threatens at all times to penetrate into full consciousness. This fear is so basic and so horrible, far exceeding the fear of death, that it is not faced by mankind.

But how does one come to be and thus gain the power for living? Victor Frankl asserts that all of mankind is searching for the meaning of life and that this meaning is a primary ingredient for the survival of personhood (Frankl, 1998). Abraham Maslow sees "self actualization" as the desired outcome in his developmental model, an exciting concept that formed the basis for the "Human Potential Movement" (Cerny, 1996).

Maslow believed that if the environment is right, people grow straight and beautiful, actualizing the potentials they have inherited. Such a premise somewhat resembles my own experience in practice. However, he said the only reason that people would not move well in the direction of self-actualization is that hindrances are placed in the way by society, primarily the educational system. I would include the educational system, but the process of derailment begins in the pre-school years and is powered more by parents than by teachers.

Eric Erickson points to such holdbacks as shame and doubt; guilt; role confusion; and despair (Kottler and Brown, 1992). Conversely, he believes trust, autonomy, initiative, industry, identity, intimacy, generativity, and integrity to be the markers of successful development. Such qualities cannot be denied as measures of maturity; however, arriving at these levels is an ideal that few achieve. Late maturity, he postulates, brings the realization of wisdom and a period of reflection about life or the regret over lost opportunity. On this last point, we are in absolute agreement.

Many have considered the words, "what might have been" the saddest in human experience. The popular duo Simon and Garfunkel sing, "A bad day is when I lie in bed and think of what might have been."

According to my experience, discovering one's "mission" in life helps describe more than anything else who one really is. While Christians might refer to the concept as a "calling", and others may term it "destiny", it is essential that every individual have a sense of having a life purpose, whether of value to one's creator (if such a belief is held), to society, or simply one's self. For many, the purpose of becoming can be the mere capacity to enjoy life fully by discovering and then celebrating who they are.

If one compares the brain to a computer, as in artificial intelligence, the slogan of programmers, "garbage in, garbage out," is illustrative. It can be seen that the human mind, when inaccurately "programmed", produces thinking and reacting that consist of "cognitive malfunctions". It might be crudely said that the brain that registers false information has a "software" problem.

Some, and perhaps many, forms of mental illness, whether a simple adjustment disorder or deep, chronic mental illness of major proportions, originate with a skewed or totally false sense of self. It is the mislearning during the developmental years that leads to psychopathology in many cases. The reason is that the adopted self, operating on false information, has too little power to stand up to the challenges of life or to maintain orderly direction.

Now, before the critics begin to pounce, let me say clearly that my premise applies to "many" psychological disorders, not to "all." Human beings are far too complicated to explain in terms of any one theory. Further, as psychology continues to take its place among the recognized sciences, having long-ago graduated from being mere philosophy, genuine research in countless areas will provide ongoing information about the human psyche and the interrelatedness between body and mind.

What I do mean to say is that the acquisition of misinformation has been largely overlooked in the etiology of mental illness and therefore should be included as an exploration that could provide a major contribution to personality theory and psychopathology. There is some precedent in the "cognitive psychology" of Beck and Ellis. Ellis's false beliefs and Beck's core beliefs dovetail with this idea.

Moving back to our model of development, we can see that an infant has no sense of becoming; that is, no sense of the development of self. From 2 to 6, however, the child explores the world of fantasy, an unbridled journey into activities, wishes and imaginings that are uncensored by whether they are possible or not. Here we see the true self fully expressed in thousands of ways. Through all this activity of mind and body, the child celebrates unrestricted being. There are no limits in the beginning period of this stage of development, and only few limits all the way to the end of this stage. This period holds the primary clues as to who the person is. The child, during this age period, and the preceding, is the true self.

These stages, however, are highly vulnerable. Abuse at this time has more devastating consequences than at any other, because the self is fully exposed, without protection. The self is open to receiving all information through sensation and through words.

While the infant has no sense of power, the young child acquires a "taste" of power as he experiences how people, objects, and his own body respond to his own will. This taste leads to a "sense" of power.

The sense of power extends into the next stage, 6 to 13, where power must be constrained through outside influences, for example, discipline. But the child, while forced to submit to restrictions, maintains his belief that his power is unlimited; hence, the "illusion of power". It is here that we see little boys jumping out of trees to fly as superman. They continue to imagine, no matter how many times they fall to the ground, that a jump is coming that will lead to flight.

Boys dream of becoming firemen, doctors, policemen and karate champions. Girls "know" they will be a princess, a model, or a ballerina when they grow up. Anything and everything is possible. But as children progress through this stage, their joy of becoming increasingly fades as outside influence competes with their illusion of power and eventually wins, though only partially.

In adolescence, about age 14 to 18, and perhaps beyond, the illusion of power has not been extinguished but only confined. This power, though nebulous, remains ready for expression, and the teen is compelled to find some way to put the power back in force for real. He rebels against the authority of other people, especially parents, and enters a search to find a clear channel of expression. Besides the constraints of authority, another enemy of his power is lack of self.

The teen, driven by social pressure, must decide on an identity, true or false, that will lead to acceptance by the peer group. He has forgotten who he is, for the original self of early childhood has internalized so much information, accurate and inaccurate, that the self barely whispers. The adolescent must pick and choose to find an identity to "try on for size." These years are, then, a period of experimental power and experimental becoming.

The adopted self of adulthood is a combination of the earlier expressed opinions of others plus the experimental choosing of a personality in late adolescence. The sense of becoming has been compromised by this conglomeration of mostly inaccurate information. If the experimental personality has become a comfortable fit, the illusion of power will return. If the fit is uncomfortable, unworkable, or in dire contrast to the true self, an illusion of powerlessness will result.

Power and Self-Esteem

An illusion of power will result in a seeming self-confidence, while the illusion of powerlessness will give birth to a feeling of helplessness. An adult with seemingly high self esteem and an adult with seemingly low self esteem are equally deluded, since neither sense is based on truth.

High self esteemers tend to accomplish more in life by the world's standards, but in times of crisis, they are just as vulnerable to psychopathology as are low self esteemers. In the stock market crash of 1929, it was the successful who leapt out of windows to their deaths. Under-achievers were in a much safer place, with much less to lose materially.

The roots of ambition are to stave off the fear of annihilation of self. The continual attainment of material things forms walls of false security around this fear. One worn-out man who came to me complained, "Everybody thinks I've got it made when they see my big house with two beautiful cars in the driveway. But they don't know what I have to go through to keep them."

I saw the man several years later and learned that instead of working on the discovery of his true self—the only way to real security—he had spent his efforts in a new business and had become a millionaire. He boasted, "I'm in multilevel marketing." When and if the pyramid scheme collapses, he will have a long fall, which could destroy him.

Many people are too busy getting further lost to ask directions. They go in circles, but they move quickly. Some rush toward the goal their parents have set; some continue a family tradition by taking over their father's business; others stalk a career they think they may enjoy or chase fantasies; and some do practically nothing. Some are financially successful and yet miserable, and some are just miserable without all the pretense. Many are convinced they don't deserve any better than what they have.

Young people set the course of their lives not by seeking their true identity but by imitating their peers, adopting TV advertising propaganda at a deep, permanent level, and taking to themselves the ethics promoted on radio and in the movies. They purchase icons in the form of clothing labels, and take their contempt for parents to the classroom, where they are encouraged in more defiance by their classmates. They placate themselves with the illusion of power, with the belief that they already know all that is worth knowing, so that there is nothing more to be learned.

Both teens and adults miss the minimal educational requirements for a fulfilling, meaningful life when they fail to discover who they are. An ecstatic preacher, at the pinnacle of his sermon, shouted to the faithful, "You are the Pearl of Great Price." But these words only deepen the sorrow of a person without a sense of being. They feel they are the exception. Perhaps every other person on Earth fits in with this wonderful claim, but not them. What, then, can be done for the man who seems to hate himself or the woman whose mind can't be changed that she's not worthy to live?

A partial answer for many forms of psychopathology is to look back and dissect the false information conveyed early in life and then to rediscover self through exploring hidden talents and abilities. The self has been covered up but not destroyed. The self cannot be destroyed but only concealed.

A beginning is to work on recalling who we were at the earliest times, before the product was tampered with, and by seriously trying out all the character traits, wishes, dreams, and fantasies of our child. This process, under the guidance of an insight-oriented therapist, is a start toward wholeness. This attainment, in most cases, is possible, regardless of age, because the child within us is unchangeable. Many believe this child is eternal.

| 3 | Lies Implanted By Abuse | |

Of all the horrid ramifications of child abuse and neglect, the self-beliefs formed by the child reap the greatest destruction. Abuse is the most penetrating and permanent communication possible, and it always conveys to the child one or more of several messages:

- "I caused it to happen." (Power or the illusion of power, depending upon the developmental stage)
- "It's my fault because I am bad." (False information internalized, encapsulated)
- "I don't deserve any better." (Erroneous judgment about self)

Sexual Abuse

The most frequent type of maltreating female children by far is sexual abuse. Whether the victim is very young or a teenager, she takes deep within herself all three messages above and develops a loathing that is all-consuming. Set up by either the taste or illusion of power, the girl concludes that there is indeed something horrible and detestable within her that caused the older person to perform such an act upon her. She knows little else but this: She is the one to blame.

Taking on the blame, however, does not explain the incident. The event makes no sense. Therefore, as a computer cannot process illogical inputs, the human mind, whether child or adult, cannot deal with events that make no sense. There is no resolution because there is no logic.

Since intelligent people tend to force sense into an occurrence so that it can be processed, the child tries to solve the mystery experimentally. A child molested early in life will be repeatedly drawn to the subject of sex, so much so that a seductive quality will seem to exude from the person until, if ever, the puzzle is put together. In addition, the victim will reflect a woundedness that is easily spotted by a predator. This is certainly one pattern. If I see a pre-teen with sexualized behavior, I know I am looking at a sexual abuse victim. However, there are other typical reactions. One is the overweight girl who dresses dowdy. Another is the Amazon warrior out to fight the world.

Because child molesters, as well as rapists, are predators, they have a capacity beyond the usual to recognize easy prey. Just as a hawk will circle above until it finds a wounded animal and then suddenly sweep in for the kill, a human predator acts in much the same way. This almost paranormal ability of human predators, combined with the woundedness of the victim, explains why, in so many cases, a child once molested will be molested again, and a woman once raped, will be raped again. I don't think this field of human activity is any different from some others. The same is true for school/workplace bullying and for violent crimes such as robberies. It can all be quite adequately explained by nonverbal signals sent out by the victim-to-be. A school bully will prod at everyone. Those who respond with emotion of any kind (fear, tears, aggression) provide amusement, so will be attacked. Those who shrug it off are left alone. The same is true regarding sex.

Molested children are very often driven to sexual activity, seemingly on a voluntary basis, in order to find some meaning in the original event. For children, mysteries demand action to solve them.

The teen years, especially the early teens, soon after maturation, bring sexual acting-out behavior in order to figure out the meaning of the earlier victimization. She is not conscious of what is urging this sexual intensity as she violates her own values and morals for more experience; that is, more chances to solve the puzzle.

Before full adulthood, she will accept a significant relationship with a male who does not exceed what she unconsciously believes she deserves (message 3, above).

Her partner will be physically and emotionally abusive, seeking to possess her in place of loving her. When she cannot stand the suffering anymore, or when there is intervention by a protective-services agency, she may be able to break the relationship, although the partner will continue to pursue her. But if she does break the tie, she will then go on to settle for another relationship that is worse than the first. Such is the case because the first confirmed what she "knew": that she deserved the treatment she received.

Because domestic violence shelters provide only protection and no effective therapy, their clientele nearly always return to the same man or find a more abusive one. The second relationship further confirms the original message, and therefore leads to still another arrangement with more severe punishment, and on and on.

Often the victim will have blocked the memory of the first assault, especially if she had been in a state of dissociation ("not there") at the time. In one case two sisters, who slept in the same bed and were molested nightly by their father, were talking. The younger sister related, "It wasn't the dark I was afraid of. It was what would come out of it." The second sister replied, "What do you mean? Didn't you ever learn to go away?"

This "going away" mentally is one form of dissociation and is a frequent "escape" from the intolerable and inexplicable. Dissociation and "repression" (the unconscious work of keeping a memory out of consciousness) are two of the reasons why child victims, and sometimes adolescent or adult victims, cannot recall the violation. However, the event does get expressed, as described above and as follows.

A 31-year-old mother found herself one morning standing in front of her dressing room mirror while holding a .38 revolver to her temple. Her finger was on the trigger, and it took every ounce of her will not to fire the gun. The urge had come seemingly from no-where, without warning. She had never had such feelings before and had never been symptomatic of any psychological disorder. Had she told any of her many friends about the incident, they would not have believed her.

What was the cause of this strange happening? She had suddenly, for some reason, recalled the horror of being sexually abused as a young girl.

All during early treatment, she carried a blank look on her face; she was expressionless. She was emotionally numb.

Part of her knew her memory was correct, while another part doubted that such would even be conceivable. So she confirmed the truth by talking to a family member—an act that required admirable courage, perhaps even heroic. To my amazement, she required very little therapy after discovering the facts.

Her case, however, is very unusual. Because her sense of self was more intact than that of many people, she possessed an inner strength that enabled her to rapidly move past her trauma. Most victims require very gentle and slow-moving therapy in order to arrive at the place she achieved so quickly. Also, she had the advantage of being molested only once, while a high percentage of victims, as stated previously, are assaulted repeatedly by other offenders following the first wounding.

This woman was also spared having to go through "therapy" as a child. Many times, when a protective-services agency discovers such abuse, the agency multiplies the trauma by tearing apart the family and forcing the child into counseling by a minimally trained paraprofessional. The so-called therapy leads nowhere but continues for years.

Unless treatment is performed by a professional who is knowledgeable about the effects of abuse, the result is that the wound is driven deeper and made wider. Her condition is worsened by endless talking about, reliving, playing out, and otherwise keeping the violation fresh, alive, and full of energy. In addition, as with any therapy in which a child is the focus, the child takes on yet another false message: "There's something wrong with me." Therapy, therefore, must be gentle, focused, and limited by a time-frame with definite goals.

By means of therapy as brief as possible, the child must be brought to an understanding that she (or he) is not at fault and is not dirty or evil. The belief that "There is something deep and dark within me that caused it to happen" must be overcome by presenting the actual facts of the matter at a pace and in a manner that the child can tolerate. The child must come to accept that the blame lies with the perpetrator only, and that children do not have the power to manipulate adults to do horrible things. Treatment that goes beyond these types of understandings further victimizes the child. Any additional therapy should be at the choice of the victim, when she reaches maturity and can decide for herself whether further attention would be helpful.

An exception to the brief approach is family therapy, which is needed when the child is presented as the source of all the family's problems. The child can be relieved in this kind of bind only by treating the family members who would otherwise escape dealing with their own issues. Blaming a child for marriage problems or other family difficulties is a form of abuse in itself.

In my experience, a little girl molested by her father or step-father is often blamed by her mother, though not always consciously. The result, however, is that the girl is doomed to live out her developmental years in the midst of maternal hostility. Although it is usually veiled, the child can sense the mother's anger and jealousy. It can be imagined with little difficulty how emotional abandonment by Mother shakes the very foundations of the child's perceived worth.

Sexual abuse of boys

Not very far behind the prevalence of female child sexual abuse is the same type of assault upon boys. Hopper (1996) estimates that about one in six boys is molested before age 16. Through extensive interviews with male survivors, Lisak (1994) found that the impact of the event correlates with the increase in age difference between the victim and perpetrator—also with the subjective emotional reaction of the child; that is, the child's perception of what was happening. He has obtained many dramatic self-reports substantiating the following themes:

- Anger
- Fear
- Homosexuality issues
- Helplessness
- Isolation and alienation
- Legitimacy
- Loss
- Masculinity issues
- Negative childhood peer relations
- Negative schemas about self
- Problems with sexuality

Other researchers (Briere et al, 1988; Fromuth, 1989; Hunter, 1991; Olson, 1990) have used standardized measurements confirming the following symptomatology:

- Anxiety
- Depression
- Dissociation
- Hostility and anger
- Impaired relationships
- Low self-esteem
- Sexual dysfunction
- Suicide attempts

Therapists working with men who were sexually abused in childhood have conducted clinical case studies (Lew, 1988; Myers, 1989) and consistently reported findings on long-term problems, including the following:

- Guilt and self-blame
- Low self-esteem
- Problems with intimacy
- Sexual problems, compulsions, and dysfunctions

- Substance abuse
- Depression
- Symptoms of post-traumatic stress disorder

Myers and other clinicians have observed confusion about sexual orientation; fear that the sexual abuse has caused or will cause homosexuality; and homophobia, an irrational fear or intolerance of homosexuality.

Every child, male or female, is vulnerable to sexual abuse, almost always committed by someone trusted by the child: parent, sibling, other relative, family friend, or caretaker (Grohol, 1996). This kind of offense includes more than the obvious touching or penetration and covers such perverse acts as exposing children to adult sexual activity or pornographic movies and photographs. Also included are having boys pose, undress, or perform in a sexual fashion on film or in person. Being spied on in the bathroom or bedroom is another offense. In short, sexual abuse is forcing or tricking a child into sexual awareness or activity for the personal pleasure of an adult or older child (Grohol, 1996).

Listed as some of the many forms of prolonged suffering that endures long after the event are (Grohol):

- Sleep disturbance
- Headaches
- School problems
- Withdrawal from family, friends, or usual activities
- Excessive bathing or poor hygiene
- Return to younger, more babyish behavior
- Running away
- Eating disorders
- Passive or overly pleasing behavior
- Self-destructive behavior
- Sexual activity at an early age
- Copying adult sexual behavior
- Persistent sexual play with other children, themselves, toys, or pets

- Displaying sexual knowledge, through language or behavior, that is beyond normal for the age
- Unexplained pain, swelling, or bleeding
- Urinary infections
- Sexually transmitted diseases

The Bottom Line of Any Type of Abuse

So far, I have discussed mainly sexual abuse, but abuse of any kind has dire consequences for the growing child. Let me interrupt in order to explain further to shed more light as my observations continue.

Whether the victim is male or female, and no matter what the constellation of resulting symptoms, the deepest ramification of any abuse, including neglect, is the disruption or derailing of the developmental process. The child is led down a blind alley when abused. If the assault takes place in the age range of 2-6, the child is blocked from exploring his true self, with the result that he will not attain the critical grasp of his own personhood before that personhood gets further modified by outside influence. Therefore, future influence which might modify can mangle instead.

Tampering with the developing self in the period 6-13 robs the child of the illusion of power necessary for his personhood to survive the subordination period of that stage. Violations in early adolescence introduce a completely false personality at a time when the teen is already experimenting with trial identities; in other words, the adolescent is denied his own choosing of what will become part of the adopted self of adulthood. Thus, the adopted self will be farther from the truth than it would be if the child were able to experiment normally.

Whatever the developmental model, abuse of any kind, if severe enough, alters the personality at the deepest levels and shakes the foundations of self development. If we look, for example, at Erikson's trust versus mistrust stage (Erikson, 1996), which is infancy, it is readily seen that even neglect, rather than direct assault, will result in the infant's learning that the world is a hostile place and that his own efforts to get his needs met produce no result. Neglect can be as damaging as the worst forms of positive abuse. The same applies to the next age level, 2-6 years, with the further impact that shame and doubt will interfere with the struggle toward autonomy.

Abuse at any of Erikson's stages will disrupt the growth of self, both at that stage and on through succeeding stages, since a child cannot progress successfully until the conflicts of a particular stage are resolved (Freud, 1996). Thus, a child denied his basic needs in infancy cannot adequately explore autonomy later on. Guilt will override initiative at 4-5, inferiority will conquer industry at 6-11, and role confusion will cloud identity at 12-18 (Erikson).

The same principle holds true with my own model of the adopted self. The self of age 2-6 cannot be explored without the strength gained through the meeting of basic needs in infancy. The true self might then be nearly extinguished, instead of just subordinated later (6-13), and there may be little remnant of self in adolescence to direct the necessary experimentation of becoming. If the sense of power is denied in infancy, the child is robbed of the taste of power later (2-6), as well as the illusion of power (6-13), and experimental power in adolescence.

A developmentally disrupted child is doomed as an adult either to accept an adopted self that has little resemblance to the true self or, in extreme cases, to invent an imaginary self. The latter might explain at least one origin of psychosis. While mere symptoms, such as anxiety or depression are caused by misinformation along the road of development, psychoses are the result of the wholesale denial of power and the nearly complete removal of any chance to discover one's self.

Secrecy

Children are abused in secret, for the most part, and are often issued dire warnings not to tell. Under-reporting by health-care providers is a continuing problem. Pediatricians, family practitioners, and other professionals sometimes wonder whether there is enough evidence to warrant the reporting of child abuse or neglect. Even though a mere suspicion justifies ethical action, facts are usually scant, and the professional is either repulsed by the idea of tearing a family apart needlessly or is in fear of a lawsuit. Again, very often children tell no-one about their being exploited sexually, physically, or mentally.

When it comes to mental abuse, and sometimes physical, the child may not be aware that anything is abnormal about the way he is treated at home. Indeed, many highly abusive parents are proud of their parenting skills and see nothing wrong with their treatment of their kids. Same is true of many abusive teachers etc. The above factors plus the three messages described earlier make one wonder how prevalent abuse is in reality. The statistics cannot possibly be accurate but are certain to be far below the actual case. Obviously, a method is needed by which to help confirm suspected abuse.

The screening test beginning on p. 38 has been developed to overcome threats and other fierce intimidation that typically prevent a child from revealing the truth about past or present suffering. This is accomplished by basing the first half of items on symptoms rather than on reputed fact recalled from memory. The child is thus able, for the first half, to answer without fear.

The symptoms included have been derived from the general literature that deals with symptoms of abuse and emotional trauma. The assumption is made that since child abuse is traumatizing, symptoms of trauma will be present when abuse has in fact occurred.

For a reason yet unknown, when children take this test, they tend to begin talking freely during the second half, when the questions are plain and obvious to the child.

A second purpose of this instrument is to provide a means for interviewing the child directly, rather than through a third party or subjective psychological tests.

This approach, because it is objective, tends to hold up in court proceedings, whereas subjective measures such as projective tests, drawings, or diagnoses made through play, call for an opinion of the expert witness. A subjective opinion by an expert witness, no matter how prominent, does not hold up well to cross-examination.

The inventory is designed primarily for use by child protective services agencies and forensic psychologists and psychiatrists, as well as by litigation support specialists working under an attorney. However, all of the following should be equipped with such a measurement:

- Attorneys
- Child protective agencies
- State Attorneys' offices
- Forensic mental-health professionals
- Domestic violence shelters
- Pediatricians
- Emergency departments
- Child psychologists
- Family practice physicians
- Psychiatric hospitals and hospital departments of psychiatry
- Community mental health centers
- City victim services agencies

Test for Concealed Child Abuse

1. I go hide so certain people won't find me.

2. I freeze in place and don't move for a while.

3. I roll up in a ball on the floor or in bed.

4. I lose the look on my face, and nobody can tell if I'm happy or sad.

5. I bang my head against the wall, on the back of my bed, on the floor, or on the back of the car seat.

6. Some adults have magic powers.

7. Some parents have magic powers.

8. My parents have magic powers.

9. Some adults can read your mind.

10. My parents can read my mind.

11. My parents have control over me even when they're not present.

12. My parents keep me away from other kids.

13. My parents never let me stay overnight anywhere.

14. I daydream or stare off into space, not really looking at anything.

15. I forget what I'm doing.

16. I don't feel pain when something should hurt.

17. I feel afraid but don't know why.

18. I feel guilty and ashamed, like I ought to be punished, even when I haven't done anything.

19. I get mad enough to break things.

20. I feel like a witch, or a vampire, or a snake, or a rat.

21. I try very hard to be perfect.

22. My parents are perfect.

23. I get real mad at some adults.

24. I get real mad at my parents.

25. I like to be close friends right away with grownups I've just met.

26. I have trouble sleeping.

27. I have trouble eating.

28. I sleep too much.

29. I eat too much.

30. I have aches and pains that people don't really understand.

31. I feel afraid, mad, sad, and guilty all at once.

32. I feel like hurting myself on purpose.

33. I have hurt myself on purpose.

34. I do things that are dangerous, where I will probably get hurt.

35. I am afraid to tell the truth about what somebody did to me.

36. I have been told by someone never to tell what happened.

37. Somebody touched my private parts, but I'll never say who it was.

38. Somebody hurt my private parts, but I'll never say who it was.

39. The person I won't tell on is an adult.

40. The person I won't tell on is an older child.

41. Certain people make me feel ashamed or bad or weird.

42. I share secrets with another person.

43. The person I share secrets with is an adult.

44. The person I share secrets with is an older child.

45. I am very afraid to tell the truth about what happened to me or about what I saw or heard.

46. I would get in terrible trouble if I told the truth.

47. Someone might be hurt or even killed if I tell the truth.

48. A pet would be killed if I tell the truth.

49. I want to tell the truth but I can't.

50. I would tell the truth if I could protect other people.

51. The people I would have to protect are:_____.

While this inventory has been greatly useful in my own practice, a comprehensive reliability and validity study has yet to be performed. Such a subject would be excellent for a master's or doctoral thesis.

Epidemic Proportions of Abuse

All of the following facts are directly from the U.S. Department of Health and Human Services (1996, 1997) and a Gallup Poll Report (1995):

- Investigations by child protective service (CPS) agencies in 49 states determined that just under 1 million children were victims of substantiated or indicated child abuse and neglect in 1997.

- In 1997, CPS agencies investigated an estimated 2 million reports alleging the maltreatment of almost 3 million children. More than half of all reports alleging maltreatment came from professionals, including educators, law enforcement and justice officials, medical and mental health professionals, social service professionals, and child-care providers. About 25 percent of these reports came from relatives of the child or from the child himself. Reports from professionals are more likely to be substantiated than reports from nonprofessional sources.

- More children suffer neglect than any other form of maltreatment. Investigations determined that about 56 percent of victims in 1997 suffered neglect, 25 percent physical abuse, 13 percent sexual abuse, 6 percent emotional maltreatment, 2 percent medical neglect, and 11 percent other forms of maltreatment. Some children suffer more than one type of maltreatment.

- Child abuse and neglect affect children of all ages. Among children confirmed as victims by CPS agencies in 1997, more than half were 7 years of age or younger, with about 26 percent younger than 4. About 27 percent of victims were children ages 8-12; another 23 percent were youth ages 13-18.

- Case-level data from 16 states suggest that the majority of victims of neglect and medical neglect were younger than 8, while the majority of victims of other types of maltreatment were age 8 or older.

- Both boys and girls experience child maltreatment. In 1997, about 52 percent of victims were female, and 48 percent were male.

- Many more children suffer abuse than are reflected in national statistics. Based on reports received and investigated by CPS agencies in 1997, about 13.9 children per 1,000 under 18 were found to be victims. In 1993, according to various community professionals, 42 children per 1,000 were harmed or endangered by abuse or neglect. A 1995 telephone survey of parents conducted by the Gallup Poll showed that as many as 49 children per 1,000 suffered physical abuse, and 19 per 1,000 were victims of sexual abuse.

Other authorities speak openly about alarm. In 1990, the U.S. Advisory Board of Child Abuse and Neglect declared the maltreatment of children to be a national emergency (Durfee, 1994). The board's chairperson, Deanne Durfee, proclaimed the tragic reality that each year hundreds of thousands of our nation's children are "starved and abandoned, severely burned and beaten, raped and sodomized, berated and belittled." They are also killed.

But most maltreatment is nonfatal. In 1992, fewer than 2,000 of the nearly 1 million abused children in the country were killed (Alexander, 1994). The numbers are nonetheless staggering. A subculture of "non-persons"—individuals stripped of their personhood—is gaining in population. Add to this the huge number whose parents habitually use put-down statements, or use conditional love as a disciplining tool.

4	# Physical Abuse	

Head Injury

The leading cause of death among abused children is head injury. But again, most child abuse victims in general do not die. Most children, 70 percent, whose head injuries are correctly diagnosed and documented have had previous head injuries (Smith, 1994). Wilbur Smith asserts,

> It is reasonable to assume, therefore, that some children's brain injuries are never detected and that there is a large degree of underdiagnosis, with an unknown number of children suffering subclinical abusive head injury, making published prevalence data artificially low.
>
> The mortality figures are merely the tip of the iceberg in measuring the pain inflicted by abuse. In most serious cases, the majority of children... suffer permanent neurological deficits. Even for those who survive without gross perceptible deficit, the outcome is not necessarily clear. Some of the "softer" signs of neurological injury, such as attention-deficit disorders, may result owing either to the injury or the chaotic environment that facilitated the abuse in the first place...
>
> Furthermore, we do not have any prior knowledge of the intellectual potential before injury... Did the injury knock 20 points off the I.Q. of a genius, rendering that child only high average?

These are usually very small children, from infancy through elementary school. Many cannot or will not talk. But what is the message about self when the person a child counts on the most in the trust-versus-mistrust stage strikes a blow to the head or throws the child across the room, down the stairs, or against the wall? The answer is that trusting is life-threatening. A message entering the mind so early in life has permanency due to its deep implantation. The child also concludes about the abuser: "He/she wants me dead." Even more devastating is the resultant belief that "If this adult wants me dead, then I don't deserve to live."

Exploration of the true self is halted as the false self begins to take over; both power and sense of becoming are suspended or removed. When a child is thus battered, he never wonders whether something might be wrong with the abuser. He always takes deep within himself the belief that there is something wrong with him.

A man in my care, Sam, now in his late 30s, lives under a bridge and eats from trash bins whenever he relapses in his struggle with alcohol. As a child, he was punched in the head routinely by his alcoholic father, for whom he holds no ill feelings. Since early adulthood, he has been billy-clubbed by police when resisting arrest as a vagrant. He holds no malice toward the police.

Periodically he detoxes and begins recovery at a halfway house that requires gradually increasing responsibilities as part of his program. When these duties reach a certain performance level, he becomes overwhelmed and confused, due to massive brain damage. He gets depressed and then full of both fear and rage. Then he drinks and returns to his "home" under the bridge.

A keen intelligence is evident early in his recovery efforts when he is neat, clean, and bright. Sam then shows a warm, friendly and cheerful spirit. When I look in his eyes, I know there is a person in there—a real one. But this man is totally unaware of who he is. His potential, probably very great before the brain damage, is untapped. Rather than clinging to an adopted self, as most people do, he has no sense of self. The early message that he does not deserve to live is blindly obeyed globally and is much too powerful and deep to be overcome for long.

Another man, Greg, in the same age group suffered regular childhood punishments of having his head slammed on the concrete floor by a crazed mother, after which he would be repeatedly taken to the hospital. Whatever brain damage did result, has not, surprisingly, completely stopped his intellectual development. The damage must have been localized by the head being stricken at the same site with every assault.

He has vivid memories of his mother parading around nude in front of him and his younger brother. He remembers being awakened in the mornings by his brother's moaning as Mother performed fellatio. He recalls sensing from early childhood through adolescence that his mother wanted him sexually, as well as his brother. As a teen, when he was dressed up to go out, the mother would comment, with a heavily seductive tone, "You look so nice."

One time in childhood when a new female acquaintance told him that he looked nice, Greg "flipped out" with rage and wanted to kill her. In this man's case, his most pervasive problem to date is rage against women, for every woman is a symbol of Mother.

His adopted self has two prominent features: "I am a sex machine humiliating women through conquering them sexually," and "I am an alien in this world without the authority to exist." His rage at times drives him near suicide, but the urge to self-destruct has been tempered through the realization that in his case, suicide would be substitute murder, the ultimate "gotcha." He has fantasies of pistol-whipping his mother.

The difference between Sam and Greg is striking. Although their abuse was similar, the effects are very different, as Greg uses his rage to survive and refuses to give up on life even though his adopted self tells him he doesn't belong on Earth. Their constitutions, being vastly different, add credence to the work of Gesell individuality at each stage of development (Bechler and Hudson, 1986).

Greg has reached, and is succeeding in, the fourth developmental stage of Piaget (1932), in which intelligence is demonstrated through the logical use of symbols representing abstract concepts. The patient is an engineering student, now studying advanced calculus. Also, he is now aware, after some treatment, that women are symbols of Mother. Thus he now manipulates these people-symbols mostly in fantasies and not nearly as much in reality. In no way does this arrangement constitute a complete recovery, but it is an improvement over the actual humiliation of women driven by the compulsion to conquer on an on.

He did, until recently, have a long-term serious relationship with a woman who was "pathologically therapeutic" for him. Married previously for 11 years to an extremely abusive alcoholic, she had a continuing false need for punishment due first to some unknown early abuse and fortified by her marriage to the alcoholic. Thus she "triggered" her boyfriend by being jealous and seductive, just as his mother had been. He called her a "whore, bitch," and worse, by using the most destructive terms he could think up. Then he suffered crushing remorse and thus returned to her. She would forgive him, and then they would repeat the cycle.

The benefit to both was that the relationship provided a release. The unwritten agreement stipulated that neither would be physically hurt and that they would not abandon each other. They would continue to cooperate for each other's benefit. Thus the pathology of each was played out in a controlled setting under fairly clear rules. The "game" worked so well, however, that each continued to endure the extreme suffering, and they did not move on in their development as individuals. Many months of treating them both were required before they were able to separate.

In order to progress beyond this developmental-arrest period, they were required to disobey the messages of childhood. Children are taught above all else to obey. Rejecting the early programming constitutes betrayal and is thus unthinkable.

Shaken Baby Syndrome

The early clinical diagnosis of this abuse is usually obscured by a fallacious history reported by the parents or caregivers. In one study, over 95 percent of the initial histories supplied by the caretakers were false. According to Wilbur Smith (1994),

> We have received a correct initial history in very few cases, and even in those cases the extent of trauma was minimized. The specious history often features a fall or choking event, rather than the true cause.
>
> The initial diagnosis is also confused because the child often presents in a state of extreme physical distress, near death. The life support activities and immediate concerns of trying to revive the child and ensure survival take precedence over careful... documentation of bruising, and establishing the definite diagnosis."
> He warns doctors not to be misled by reports of short falls less than four feet.
>
> Serious injuries take serious trauma, and a child with serious head injury who is not involved in an automobile accident or a fall from several stories should be considered a possible victim of child abuse in the process of differential diagnosis.

It is clear that an injury of this kind requires real violence—ruthless, hateful behavior against a child in the first developmental stages. At a time when he is testing the safety of his environment, he finds excruciating punishment without cause, totally unpredictable, unrelated to his own actions. He learns that crying for his needs to be met or crying because he is already in pain will lead to further pain.

Such a message, internalized at the earliest time, is implanted permanently. "I am helpless." "Nothing I try will work." "I will be punished for anything I try to do." "It is wrong and dangerous to get my needs met." Such communication will be the data base to be struggled against as the child later seeks his personhood. The true self will be tightly constricted in its expression, and the base-line information will under-gird each developmental stage thereafter.

The taste of power of toddlerhood, so necessary to propel later efforts, will be severely minimized if not obliterated. The illusion of power in the elementary-school years will be replaced with underlying fear of people and the global realm of the unknown. The experimental becoming of adolescence will be carried out, if at all, with great timidity. The adopted self, in the end, will be one of powerlessness.

Abdominal Injuries

This classification of child abuse is second only to head injuries in mortality. According to Dirk Huyer (1994), "High mortality rates in cases of inflicted thoracoabdominal trauma may be explained in a variety of ways. Delay in medical treatment results from delay in presentation, inaccurate or misleading historical information provided by parents, and lack of information from the child. Because these features are frequently coupled with a lack of obvious external injury, a high index of suspicion is required."

It is not too harsh to conclude that there is little difference, if any, between a physical child abuser and a potential or actual murderer. These abusers are more than willing to risk the life of the child in order to conceal their venomous acts. They are murderous and full of deceit and self protection. Most are repeat abusers and do, at some level, want the child dead at the time of the crime. In many cases there are two abusers, each equally guilty, for one commits the assault and the other covers for the assailant. Parents presenting their child for treatment, if they do, confirm each other's story about what happened.

Huyer describes graphically the truth of the attack: "Direct blows crush organs against the immobile vertebral column or the lower rib cage with resultant laceration and hemorrhage. The hollow visceral organs (stomach and intestines) are filled with food, liquid, air, or stool. A direct blow compresses the contents, leading to sudden overdistension, with rupture spilling the contents into the abdominal cavity. With rapid deceleration of the body, internal partially mobile organs continue in motion with resultant tearing of intestinal mesentery."

The message to the developing child? "My body is a source of pain, not a source of pleasure." At a time when the infant or elementary-age child should be exploring and celebrating his body, he wishes he could get out of it. If he doesn't have actual physical problems on through adolescence and adulthood, he will be preoccupied with the subject. Pain in small amounts will bring fear, but he will not understand where the fear is coming from. He will not connect the present emotional distress with the earlier history of having pain inflicted on him, pain that does not go away in a few minutes but instead seems never to end. Thus, it is justifiable to ask whether such treatment is one cause of hypochondriasis.

Scourging

This category of corporal punishment includes the use of any instrument to inflict pain by whipping, whether by use of an actual whip, a switch, a belt, or another flexible weapon. Because this form of abuse is no less than torture and thus fully exposes sadism in extreme cases, and because tissue injury is visible, these victims are kept away from doctors. Otherwise, the secrecy is fairly easy to maintain, since usually the strokes are delivered to the buttocks and/or legs and are therefore out of view.

The first man I treated for post-traumatic stress disorder arising from child abuse was my most challenging, due to his inability to control his yelling and screaming during therapy. I came close to being evicted from my office building.

While Lloyd was tortured all of his life, his recollection of events at about 12 are most vivid. His mother used to command him at will, always without provocation, to go outside and select a "good" switch. The rule was that he would be assaulted all the more if he did not select one that would cause great pain. It had to be long enough and green enough, strong enough, and flexible enough.

When he returned with the switch, he was made to remove all of his clothing, even his underwear, and stand before his mother totally naked and without moving. She would then whip him until she exhausted herself. She included all parts of the body, and made certain that she hit the genitals well. She stopped only when she was completely unable to deliver another blow.

Lloyd remembers time after time trying to stand still but slipping on his own blood upon the wooden floor. When he slipped, his mother became even more enraged. After each beating, all of them without notice, the boy crawled upstairs to treat his own wounds.

One time, while still bleeding from such a session, he ran out the door and all the way to the local police station to beg for rescue. He could get no help, because one of the officers was a sexual partner with the mother.

When this man first came to me at the age of 32, he was unable to speak during our sessions but only to scream, moan, and roar in rage. He was the most frightening patient I have ever treated. From late teens until a few years ago, he was repeatedly placed in one psychiatric hospital after another, in addition to jail.

He had become addicted to both drugs and alcohol, and remained an addict for years. Never in all of his psychiatric history was he correctly diagnosed but only assigned one false label after another, including sociopath, schizophrenic, manic depressive and others. His true diagnosis from the beginning should have been "complex post-traumatic stress disorder," in my experience a condition very common to physical abuse.

After a long period of treatment, which began with daily, one-to-one sessions, and later progressed to male group therapy, this man has made a remarkable recovery. He is working full-time, living independently, and forming friendships. As a member of a very warm and supportive church, he has been working diligently on forgiving his mother. He traveled several hundred miles to see her when she was near death, and then went back again to attend her funeral.

Another man, David, now in his late 50s, still has monthly or more frequent dreams of conquering his father, who has been deceased for nearly 30 years. He remembers as a boy watching his father proudly weave two leather dog leashes together for training the family pet, a pedigree Boxer. At the end of the two woven leashes, he attached a hard, wrapped ball, somewhat larger than a golf ball, which he formed by tightly winding a long, leather thong. He left some remaining strips dangling loose off the end of the ball to resemble a cat-of-nine-tails. Even at his young age, the boy wondered why such a device would be needed to train a dog.

Not long after the project was complete, David learned that the weapon was for him. He had been accused, at age 7, of talking back to a teacher, something he had not done, as he tried repeatedly to explain to his parents. But his father took out that odd weapon. The man remembers the horror of not being able to get away, incapable of standing, trying to scurry under the kitchen sink, only to be yanked straight in the air by one arm so the father could get another series of blows in. On and on it went, until the boy believed it would continue until he was dead.

A few days later, when previously scheduled physical exams were conducted at school, the doctor asked what happened, upon seeing the black and blue stripes and shapeless wounds from the chest down. The victim said that he had fallen. The doctor did nothing. David is described at length in Chapter 10.

The developmental impact in these last two cases? In Lloyd's case, the boy had learned that any action could bring punishment. From toddlerhood to about age 6, he was unable to learn right from wrong, because pain was random, lacking any cause and effect. Rather than having his chance at trial personalities during adolescence, he did not have enough sense of self even to begin the activity. There was no experimental becoming in adolescence, for their was no imaginary power to energize the effort. His adopted self became limited to an organism that felt nothing but rage and other deep pain. As a result, this patient's personhood needed to be constructed during long, tedious, and wrenching therapy.

In David's case, the boy's developmental growth was too heavily dependent on his relationship with mother alone, for any remark or activity with the father was far too risky. The interaction that should have occurred, and the "Welcome to manhood" message that can be given only by a father never occurred. Thus, his male identity formation was weakened.

Fortunately, he became intimately involved with a female in his mid-teens, and the intense sexual relationship that ensured almost from the beginning more than confirmed his sexual orientation. He did, though, develop a seething hatred for teachers, since a teacher's false accusation led to his violent separation from his father. He became a substandard student, even though he was of very high intelligence and had performed very well in school before the event. Further, the educators who could have helped form his adopted self had less than no influence, and some of these teachers had been very gifted.

In both cases, the boys were plagued by the fact that a parent hated them. There is hardly a stronger block to self worth that the belief that a parent hates you. Any child concludes that there must be something to hate and thus carries this conviction for life. When a child has limited or no value for himself (or herself) each succeeding stage of development is colored by some degree of self-hatred, with the result that the effort to progress is half-hearted and lacking in power.

Punching and Other Violence

David, the same boy who had been wounded with the dog device, was warned that if that kind of punishment didn't work, that his father would "treat him like a man" and begin using his fists. (The father had been an amateur heavyweight boxer. He weighed about 240 pounds at about 6-foot-one.)

This child had always been taught to brutalize any other child for almost any reason, and so the boy, being fairly large for his age through junior high school, had gained a reputation for being a fierce fighter (even though he suffered tremendous guilt after hurting another child).

At about age 13, he was accused at the dinner table of doing something he had not done, and his father became insanely enraged when the boy persisted in not admitting any guilt. The father walked over to the seated child, who was just placing a fork in his mouth, and hit him in the left jaw with such force that the boy was lifted up into the air and landed in the corner of the room in a heap, momentarily unconscious.

He looked up and saw the blurred figure of his towering father standing above him with clenched fists, a red face, and yelling, "Get up, so I can hit you again. Get up!" The boy was reduced to infancy and cried loud, uncontrollably, hysterically. At that moment, he felt destroyed. His deep shame over not being able to force himself to get up and take another punch lasted well into adulthood.

David backed down from every other opportunity for a fight, even when confronted, for the rest of his teen years. One time he let another teen snatch his bicycle and ride away. He gave up playing football in junior high and in fact developed a hatred for athletes. He quit the Explorer Scouts, quit trying in school, quit all previous interests, and resolved that he would do nothing from now on unless paid. So he got a job working as a dishwasher.

A few similar attacks occurred in his later teens. His father often got right up in his face and then "sucker punch" him so that the boy would go flying across the room and

then hit the floor in a daze. The boy, almost totally deper-
sonalized, decided that he had to do something.

Hitting his father, even though he had gained the courage by self talk over the years, was unthinkable. He could
not bring himself to hit his father. He felt that was the
worst thing a son could ever do. But he did think of something that he could do that would partially restore his
male identity: He could refuse to fall down when hit, no
matter how hard. He mastered the skill of never going
down, always staying on his feet after a sucker punch. He
came right back into his father's face and continue what
he was saying, as though nothing had happened.

By about 18, the young man told his father that he was
through listening to him at all and that he had no regard
for him as a father, nor for his opinions. The victim had
made a tiny step toward becoming a man with this absolute rejection of his abuser. In a way, he had overcome his
intimidator—not by force, but by denying his father's personhood and the father's message from the earliest time
that the boy had no worth and could not become a man.

The dynamic of conquering one's abuser is one that
plays in the mind of the victim forever. Because the abuser
has robbed the victim of power, the power must be re-
gained in some manner. Hence, the endless fantasies and
dreams of overcoming the one who not only punished the
body but raped the self.

Back to the first man described, Lloyd: He had been
subjected to a very broad range of sadistic abuse in addition to what has already been said. He was locked outside
in the cold, beaten on the head with a bible as Mother
quoted condemning scriptures, and forced to revive her
each time she passed out from an asthmatic attack, usually caused by cursing at him until she'd lost her breath.

At about the age of 10, he was cooking dinner, as he
did when there was food, and he happened to put too
much spaghetti in the pot. His mother made him reach
into the boiling water with his bare hand again and again
until he had reduced the contents to the quantity she
wanted.

It is no surprise that this man's recovery in adulthood required first doing something about the indescribable rage that he had carried all his life. Never did the child have a way to express this rage in his developmental years, for he dared not let his mother know. Even worse punishment would result if he let on.

Rage, being the strongest emotion there is, must find the exactly correct outlet in order to be disposed of. Rage is pain in the true self, as is anger. When present, rage dominates both the activities and the direction of every developmental stage. Just as no-one can work while in severe physical pain, a child cannot conduct the "work" of development when crippled by pain in the self. Rage of this kind, then, not only retards growth but can literally arrest development.

This man, therefore, was in many ways a child when he first came for help. He had no control over emotions, no inner strength to accomplish the normal duties of life, and very little knowledge of the world and its people. He needed to be parented for a long time, once the rage was dealt with.

Anger, the extreme form of which is rage, is unlike other emotions in that it must be directed to the person who caused it in order for it to discharge permanently.

It is obvious that physical pain is a benefit to the body in that it protects against further injury or a worsening of the cause. Pain is a warning signal that something must be done, that an injury has occurred and that the body is in danger. So it is with the pain of anger: It is a warning that our personhood is in danger or that it has already been injured, that something must be done to restore its previous health.

Anger, or rage, is a form of pain as necessary as physical pain. When we are insulted, humiliated, treated with contempt, or treated unfairly or outrageously, we feel the pain of anger just as unavoidably as we would feel physical pain in case of a bodily injury.

While anger can be *expressed* in any number of ways, it cannot be *discharged* unless directly aimed at the offender. This is the reason why the popular anger-management classes of today are not only ineffective but harmful. They result in the client's holding down and further suppressing the very pain that is so necessary. The pain is retained rather than used in a constructive way to build the self.

However, if the offended one goes to the person who caused the pain and simply states that the action or words hurt and that he will not tolerate such an injury again, the anger (or rage) leaves, never to return. Note that the client is not required to hurt the offender but only to object.

Even when the offender is deceased, this vital task must still be accomplished. The afflicted one need only talk to the deceased as though still alive, and believe that the offender does hear. Sometimes writing a letter to a dead abuser can be effective, and the same method can be used for others who for some reason cannot be reached. Even in cases where a victim dare not contact an assailant, as in criminal cases, a letter can be written but never mailed. The healing effect is much the same as a one-on-one interaction. Even more effective is voicing one's feelings into a tape recorder, without any censorship whatsoever; at a later time it can be decided whether to send the recording.

Whatever the form of physical abuse, the results are similar, but the intensity varies according to the amount of physical pain and the amount of anger. In our society, children are beaten, whipped, punched, thrown, strangled, stabbed, molested, burned, pinched, and pummeled. To some degree, in every case, the child takes on false information and gets robbed of opportunity both in the developmental stage in which the atrocity occurs and in every subsequent stage as well.

5	# Terrorizing	

A Brother and Sister

While practicing in Philadelphia, I was presented with a brother and sister who could remember almost nothing before the age of 7. Both had suffered psychotic episodes beginning at age 15 and continuing through their 20s, with multiple hospitalizations. The sister was functioning to an extent, although heavily medicated, but she tended to get "sick" about every three to six months and required hospitalization again.

The brother was quite infantile in his thoughts and behavior and was extremely fearful and nervous all the time. Of the two, he seemed to be the most seriously damaged, yet he was the one most willing to stay in treatment, and he constantly worked very hard to move into new behaviors that were very challenging for him. Although he had been diagnosed as schizophrenic, I believed that his constellation of symptoms was trauma-induced. (The sister had been labeled "bi-polar" and thus had her "breakdowns" attributed to a chemical imbalance.)

I was unable to obtain any information from either parent in trying to find out the origins of their conditions, that is, what caused them to be this way. The mother did mention some small events in early childhood, but seemed unaware of anything major.

The father, living in a distant city, was contacted but categorically refused to offer any information of any kind. He said what would really help them is to stop all therapy and all medications. Being a long-term member of Alcoholics Anonymous, he suggested they join Al-Anon.

Both brother and sister held the conviction that they were terrorized as small children by their father, who was an active alcoholic during that time period. But neither could remember anything except being terrified of him then and in the present. They each had shadowy, vague, fragmentary glimpses of being used as experiments in the basement of their home. Their father had been a medical student in their early years, and they believed he used them for practice in a mock treatment room he had set up in the basement.

They both seemed certain that their father had a vile temper and used to scream at them and their mother. The brother thought that he himself might have been molested by a man whom he cannot recall, and the sister wondered if she might have awakened in her father's bed after having been drugged. Yet all of these images were hazy, and neither spoke with certainty. It was as though they were guessing.

At one point during treatment, I commented that both the sister and the mother tended to over-react whenever the brother got upset and, further, that he was not encouraged in accepting responsibility. Without hesitation, the sister instantly responded, as though the words were coming out by themselves, "I think Mom and I are afraid my brother will let out a family secret."

In that family, there are secrets galore. These secrets are the terror that paralyzes the victims and keeps them that way. The secrets are protected by maintaining the position that the daughter has a chemical imbalance, that the son is schizophrenic. The cover-up in this family and many others I have dealt with would falsely lead one to believe that both brother and sister are "sick" from unexplained causes that are no-one's fault and that nothing can be done except to medicate and periodically hospitalize.

Despite all of this denial, not all of which was conscious, it was evident that these patients were reliving childhood terror and that this crippling fear was maintained by the mystery of not knowing what had happened to them. Their fears and resultant powerlessness had become spooky and magical. Therefore, we began analyzing the only information we had: their delusions, hallucinations, nightmares and flashbacks, as well as their many fears.

These phenomena, though grossly disturbing to the patient, provide invaluable information. Just as analysts use dreams, full use can be made of hallucinations as well. *Every nightmare and every hallucination should be explored for symbolic or literal content,* for these representations, no matter how bizarre or seemingly nonsensical, originate in the reality of experience. The power of these frightening products of subconscious material subsides when the patient realizes that placing them in the light provides precious clues.

Through paradoxical intention, the patient moves from fearing these phenomena to regarding them as treasures that will help set him free. When this intention is applied, the true self is in control rather than the powerless adopted self, and the patient begins to experience the actuality of power while the eerie, mystical force of hallucinations and nightmares fades.

Even though we did not know the details of what had happened, we were able to piece together some conclusions that made sense to the patients and that could be processed. Neither has been hospitalized since treatment began about four years ago; their medications have been reduced; the brother has begun to seek employment; and the sister is more comfortable as a mother and wife.

Both patients are highly intelligent, and they have many abilities, but these resources will remain dormant until each discovers more truth about what was done to them. *Mystery is the great terrorist, and family secrets keep it fully alive.*

The most helpful accomplishment in this case is that these young people do not view themselves as hopelessly and mysteriously mentally ill. They now view themselves as victors instead of victims, who are yet reacting to the abnormality of someone else. There is power in their hope of discovering more about their past and thus continuing their process of becoming.

The Bedwetting Boy

In Jacksonville, Florida, I was presented with a 6-year-old boy who had undergone bladder surgery for a bed-wetting problem. His mother, who had been in psychotherapy for 30 years, had been told by her most recent psychiatrist to consult an urologist regarding his son's problem. The mother had agreed, and thus the urologist recommended and performed bladder surgery. The surgery accomplished nothing, for the problem continued unchanged.

In talking with both the mother and the boy, I discovered almost immediately that the child had been living in the fear that his father would kill both Mother and himself. He had repeatedly witnessed the father, in a drunken rage, ransacking the house and threatening to kill them, and he had watched his father grab Mother by the hair and hurl her down a flight of stairs. The boy had been wetting the bed only after each of these episodes.

One 10-year-old boy was brought to me by his mother for a second opinion. Another doctor had recommended that the child receive weekly psychoanalytic therapy through age 21.

Clearly, the boy was upset, but his "disturbance" was the direct result of what he had witnessed. He had recently returned from a visit with his estranged father in a distant state. The father was living a completely unregulated homosexual lifestyle that included parading around in the nude along with his lover and performing all sorts of sexual acts in the presence of his son. (There is no implication here whatsoever that such behavior is typical of homosexuals.)

The boy's emotions had been ransacked by this horror. He had been so terrified by this first experience of seeing grown males fully erect that he had become grotesquely sick at his stomach and wanted to run but was prevented. His emotions, heightened to the maximum, were conflicted among anger, helplessness, alienation, grief, and, of course, guilt. As every child does, he felt responsible for the debacle that had taken place.

The child's resultant needs were to understand that he was not the problem, that there was nothing wrong with him, and to be comforted as well as affirmed. Certainly no extensive therapy was required, and the child recovered very quickly, Had he not received this brief intervention, however, or had he been subjected to long-term "therapy", the impact of the trauma would have penetrated more deeply and would have become permanent.

Adolescent Cases

One mother of a 13-year-old girl was dismayed after divorcing the child's father and not being able to get her daughter to accept her new partner. The solution was to send her to boarding school. After struggling with this rejection for several weeks, the girl became noticeably depressed and was thus referred to the school's psychiatric advisor. Hospitalization was arranged immediately. Following two months of in-patient "treatment," the girl was sent home to Mother for a visit.

After the girl had been home a few days, the mother came upon a sudden realization: When her daughter was in boarding school, there were substantial costs; when she was in the hospital, the insurance company paid everything. So the mother went directly to the child and told her she wished she had never been born; that she was a hopeless case; that she never wanted to see her again. In perfect obedience, the child became very depressed and was re-admitted to the same hospital. When she began to improve under my care, she was reassigned to another doctor. She spent the greater part of her teen years, until age 18, in and out of hospitals.

Soon after I began my private practice in Philadelphia, a father brought his 15-year-old son to me. Having heard of me through a newspaper article, he was willing to travel the 150 miles to try to find out the truth about his son's condition. Before they had left to see me, the mother had called me and said, "They have my permission to see you, but I know it's not going to do any good. There's been something wrong with my son ever since he was born, and we've taken him to doctors all of his life. I've already told my husband that either he (the boy) goes, or I do."

An exhaustive interview with the father and son together convinced me that the absent one, Mother, was the one who needed treatment. For years, she had taken out her frustrations on her son and blamed him for all her problems, including the bad marriage that she herself ruled.

At the end of our one time together, I told the boy that he had been carrying a false label of "mentally ill" all of his life and that now he must remove it for good. I told him to discard the label completely and never to pick it up again. The father broke down and wept. Between sobs of relief and joy, he exclaimed, "I've always known at some level that my boy was all right, but I couldn't get anybody to agree with me."

In all of the above cases, it can be seen that these children had assimilated incorrect information about themselves. As every child does, they believed what was communicated about them, either in words or in deed, or both. By therapeutically removing the false "inputs" and reprogramming with facts, they were enabled to proceed with a more normal self development so that the adopted self of adulthood would not be further removed from reality than for many people.

Notice also, that professionals had done much to affix the label of mental illness in the first place. They had cooperated with the abuse of the parents by taking at face value the deviated histories presented by the adult caregivers. But just as parents render false reports in cases of physical abuse, they do the very same with mental abuse, especially with terrorizing. *When a doctor helps attach a false label, it takes another doctor to remove it.*

Death of a Terrorist

One of the most emotionally confusing times in the life of an abuse victim is when the victimizer dies. The victim's reaction is bewildering. While the grieving process is absolutely necessary—for mourning should occur for any major loss, even loss of an abuser—grief is clouded and conflicted with other feelings, some of which have a "magical" quality for the patient.

In order to illustrate, I have included an excerpt from an earlier work of mine (Castallo and Ewart, 1977) in which I describe for my character, a prominent physician, his own experience in seeing his abusive father lying on his deathbed.

> Powerful fathers are not easily erased from daily consciousness. And to know that the most basic influence in your life is losing his presence brings on a recurring melancholy. Salvatore [father] had always been the looming object I needed to overcome—or at least equal—so that I could be a person myself. Through his long deterioration, as hardening of the arteries usurped his acuity, I felt an occasional pull of depression without fully understanding. Perhaps I was so unsettled by the way old age and circumstance had downed my father that I lost an adolescent goal to compete with him. I was ashamed of an immature motivation to overcome him and compelled at the same time to seek strength for myself.
>
> There was nothing in the future that Salvatore could bank on. The old man had long ago issued his last command, and there had been nothing fearful in him for years. But even in his confusion he moved with a remnant of dignity. Strangers could somehow detect that the big gentleman had been somebody.
>
> Salvatore's doctor knew when to call the final visit—when to inform a close relative that death

was forthcoming and that the family must gather soon or not at all. I was notified late one evening in February, only a few months after he had gone back to Providence.

As dusk approached on the following day, I was entering the house in Providence to see my father and to say good-bye.

He was alone and still in a room that looked unvisited, and I thought at first that he might have already passed. But as I studied his large frame from the open doorway, I was both relieved and frightened to see his big chest rise slowly and descend. I walked straight over to him and saw as I approached that he was wet and that the white sheets were clinging to his sweaty, tremulous limbs. He looked like a gigantic, abandoned puppet whose strings had rotted away.

His pure-white mustache stood out as the only spirited feature on a once-commanding face—that is, until his eyes opened. His eyes! They were clear, agile, and full of activity. They seemed to live on beyond Salvatore, seemed to be waiting behind in order to gather up a final image for eternal reflection.

I studied him and memorized every aspect of his presence that I could. Then, after only another moment or two, I grasped his limp hand, kissed him on the cheek, and promised to visit him in the morning. But I knew he would be gone.

Had he been different—or had I—or maybe if we hadn't been so similar—I don't know—then I might have loved him. But I did, and I do, fear him.

6 Parentification

A fairly common practice of parents is to make the child an intermediary when a fight is going on. When parents do avoid assigning the child this role, the child will often slip into the role without prompting. *Attempting the impossible and never giving up will always result in symptoms of some kind.*

Children forced to endure parental fighting or to witness one parent being abused by the other will suffer emotional turmoil, including fearfulness, becoming withdrawn (so that he does not have to take sides), or acting out as a behavior problem in order to draw attention to himself as a decoy and stop the threatening struggle. Bed wetting, for example, or nonconformity in school, can sometimes accomplish a truce and also provide a way to vent the unavoidable rage the child feels as a result of what he is being put through.

If it isn't the marriage itself that is the source of the child's unrest, it is often another kind of unhappiness on the part of one or both parents. Every child who senses unhappiness, fear, or other distress in a parent will try to "fix" it. He will not only believe that he is able, but will actually take it upon himself as his own personal responsibility, often for life.

As already explained at length, children are not aware that their power is limited. In fact, they go through necessary stages of illusory, imagined, and experimental power (table 2-1, p. 14). Thus, children undertake the task of rescuing Mother or Father or both. They try to be a better boy or girl, perform perfectly in school (or misbehave), be quieter or noisier when Mommy's upset, go to bed earlier, stay up later, stop fighting with siblings, start fights with siblings, try something different, or try everything harder. This is to achieve the goal of happy parents who are available to meet their needs. *When they fail, and they always do, it is their fault.*

In one case of this kind, I was a young woman's 30th doctor. Laura came to me at the age of 19, never having been out of the hospital for more than six months from the time she was 13. She arrived with the firm expectation that I would put her back in the hospital, as all 29 other doctors had done.

When the entire family was called into the office, everyone showed up except the father, who had long ago abandoned them all. The patient, however, deep in her subconscious, continued to hope that repeated hospitalizations would bring him back. Through all these years, the family had deteriorated through the mother's lost ability to govern. Laura believed that they were just as "sick" as she. I agreed.

They did not need to deal with this fact, however, because they kept their focus on the patient, who cooperated fully. She was the endpoint in every matter discussed, and the family was entrenched in a process of shunning their own problems by projecting them onto the patient.

All through the first family session, Laura was the only one openly upset. She spoke with emotion, cried, complained and argued, but the rest of the family stayed composed as uninvolved observers. When all of this was pointed out, that the patient was expressing all of the emotion for them, they seemed unconvinced. I suggested that the patient felt all alone in being the only one to admit the pain, that she was crying on behalf of them all, that she was suffering in their place. This arrangement was not fair, I contended, and it was too much for the patient.

Finally, one of the brothers sprang up and ran over to comfort her. Next, a sister followed; then, Mother. Before long they were all weeping and yet with great relief because it was good to have everything out in the open.

All resistance and denial were given up by the family, and they began to talk honestly about the real causes of their suffering. The patient was relieved of her obligation to continue as "mentally sick". Instead, she began to lead her family into some deep insights about the way they had all dealt with emotional pain in the past. She never returned to the hospital.

Mixing children into parental struggles is pervasively destructive simply because children believe what their parents tell them, no matter how preposterous. They try to adapt to the role they are assigned or place on themselves. *Children will participate in any and all madness.*

A child can have a role assignment even before birth, and sometimes before conception, as in the case of a child conceived as the final effort to save a marriage. Other parents, as mentioned, conceal the hidden agenda of possessing a child for life as an emotional support. Usually a daughter is chosen as a lifetime companion, but sometimes a son is so used.

Very often, we see a sad and feeble rebellion whereby a girl so singled out may resist to a point during young adulthood, even going so far as to marry, in defiance of her "duty" to serve Mother. Such unfortunates tend to marry someone who is sure to fail as a spouse, so that a return to Mother is guaranteed. This kind of abuse occurs more frequently in single-child families.

Debbie: 20 year–old Anorexic

A woman we'll call "Debbie" came to me at age 20 after several hospitalizations for anorexia. She had long ago been convinced that she did not deserve to live and in fact had no right to live. Mother had been addicted to alcohol and prescription drugs all of Debbie's life and had always refused any kind of treatment. She had chased the girl's father out when she was in second grade and from that time on made her daughter her "mother".

All during her elementary and high-school years, Debbie was a captive in charge of making Mother happy in a contract that guaranteed a no-win. The unwritten agreement was, "It's your job to make me happy, but nothing you do will ever work." While Debbie was still in elementary school, she had branded herself as unworthy to live because she was already failing at the job she thought she was born to do.

Mother had also taught her from the earliest age that she was not permitted to pray for herself but only for her mother. "If you pray for yourself, you are being selfish."

In her late teens, Debbie had made a kind of adjustment by becoming overly dependent on a tight network of very close friends who had taken responsibility for keeping her alive. In this mode, Debbie was allowed to be the child previously forbidden to exist. They sympathized with her condition and fussed over her until she finally ate, in obedience to her surrogate parents. At times she took enough nourishment to stay alive for a little while, only to be overcome with the deep weight of failure, at which point she ceased all intake except water until she was again hospitalized.

One particular time, she had very nearly succeeded in starving herself to death, and the doctors did not know whether she would live or not. Mother came to visit her in the intensive care unit. With Debbie lying there near death, with tubes in her arms and hooked up to monitors, Mother exclaimed, "If you could just get over this, I could die in peace." Debbie did not miss the message: If she dared to recover, her mother would die.

One might reasonably wonder how such a victim could ever get free. For Debbie, the answer was the same as for everyone caught in any kind of bondage: the truth. She had to realize clearly in what ways she was acting in direct response to her mother, what her real responsibilities were, what roles were possible for her in life, and what part she had played in remaining a captive. She had to accept the fact that she must give up the impossible and begin doing the possible in every facet of her life. It was required, as terrifying as the process was, that she face the truth about what her mother had been doing to her all of her life.

Above all this, Debbie needed to discover who she was; that is, gain some clue as to her true self, a personhood having infinite value apart from any other person in the world. It had not been possible to come to a place where she could feel good about her "self" because her self had never been explored. She had to begin by discarding the false self that had gotten its power from misinformation and impossibilities; she had to drop the false self like an old coat, never to pick it up again, and start afresh in the light of fact.

A child may succeed in pleasing his parents, may make them laugh, may be a good student, may clean his room admirably, but he cannot make a parent happy or solve a parent's problems. Trying to make anyone happy, no matter what age in the developmental process, and no matter what the relationship, will create a "failure theme" with a strong component of pervasive guilt. Herein lies a major root of depression in adolescence and early adulthood.

Children of Alcoholics

The dynamic of parentification is both strong and frequent in alcoholic families. Many children of alcoholics who seek treatment in adulthood are unaware that their present distress is related to alcoholism in the family, no matter how far in the past. Most are convinced that there is inherently something wrong with them in that they cannot seem to cope, to live in peace with their intimates, or feel fulfilled in their life's work (if they have found it). In some regard, they tend to feel lost.

It must be remembered that an alcoholic in a family is a hurricane, so consistently powerful that the entire family is forced to adapt to the threat of imminent violence or a host of other forms of craziness. When a family "adapts" to craziness, they have formed a maladjustment that makes their situation seem normal. But there is no normal way for anyone to adapt to craziness.

Their ways of relating to each other, covering up the unpleasant, not talking about emotional subjects, learning to keep family secrets, all become a deep-set mode of functioning. The fall-out of such entrenchment reaches down from one generation to another to another.

As one example, it seems that the overwhelming majority of daughters of alcoholics tend to marry alcoholics,
often more than one. As women tend to do, they are seeking to find their fathers in their husbands, but in their
case Father is a risky model in picking out a mate. Nonetheless, such a young woman will recognize certain
personality traits that seem not only familiar but somehow
enticing. Her own father, always inaccessible, seems available in another body. Seeing her father in such a one, she
sees a chance to have her father at last, after all those
years of being deprived.

There can be a conflicting need for such a daughter to
gain her "father" but also at the same time to rebel against
him. She can develop an unwieldy relationship in which
both love and hate vie for the same space in her heart. In
such a dilemma, she will seem to hold on too tightly and
be prone to extreme jealousy and yet at the same time be
subject to the sudden powerful urge to reject or punish
her mate. She retains the deep and powerful need for her
father along with an equally powerful need to vent her rage
against him. Yet these emotions will be pushed aside when
the alcoholic drinking pattern in her husband emerges—if
the marriage lasts that long—and she will undertake again
what has always eluded her: getting him to stop drinking.
When she fails, it will be her fault.

The term "she" continues to be used here, for indeed it
is most often a woman who comes for help when caught in
this kind of a life-limiting problem. Certainly young men
have been caused to suffer in similar ways, but they tend
to handle their problems in a manner that usually remains
outside the doctor's office. For example, when the husband
is an adult child of an alcoholic and is playing out the
consequences on his wife, whether knowingly or not, he
will usually send his wife to the doctor. This is a trait of
men in general, no matter what kind of problem prevails.
Husbands, regardless of their role in the difficulties, all too
often tell their wives, "You go. You're the one who thinks
there's a problem."

A girl growing up in an alcoholic family will often be doomed to failure regardless of which parent is the drinker. She will be the peacemaker and the one who tries to protect one parent from the other. All during her developmental years, she hopes that if she tries harder, then Mom or Dad will change. Any child caught up in such a bind will eventually take on the self-appointed label of failure. Trying the impossible over a sustained period of time will produce this kind of condemnation in the adopted self, and she will likely spend a lifetime trying to overthrow the verdict. The theme will be played out on the eventual spouse and on the children, who will find that they also have a parent who cannot be made happy.

The failure identity very often leads such a child to over-achieve, first in school and later in most other kinds of challenges. They will have a tendency to become people pleasers, having failed so miserably with the most important people in their lives: their parents. They will also be prone to relationships of bondage with unreasonable, demanding, inconsistent people, sometimes tyrannical people, just like the ones at home during childhood. Sometimes they work out their early maladaption by setting the goal of becoming the ambitious, successful, family "savior", the one who finally brings some dignity to the family name. This course is the most frightening of all, because it consumes nearly all of one's energy. Failure is always right behind, no matter what the level of success, so to stop running would be unthinkable.

Because an adult child of an alcoholic has not learned what normal existence is, she (or he) must guess as she tries to make her way through life and possibly establish her own family. Whatever a child has experienced in her own family is normal for her, though by reasonable standards her "normal" might very well be crazy. A child brought up in confusion, plus the threat of imminent danger, or at the very least, constant insecurity, must seek by trial and error to discover what the real meaning of normal is. Missing what should have been learned in the family setting, plus having learned much in the way of irrationality, results in a huge learning void that must be made up for by direct, therapeutic teaching.

Such a young adult—or even a middle-aged one—will be further done in by nondirective counseling approaches that forever ask, "What do you think?" The patient is missing some vital information about what normal is, and it doesn't matter what she thinks as much as what she needs to learn. Thus, the therapist must be a patient teacher who is directive in his treatment.

These victims have difficulty following projects through to completion. They tend to shift priorities and feel that whatever they are working on at the time is the wrong thing. They have not been taught how to establish priorities because have been raised in a home where there has always been but one priority: keeping the peace and avoiding further disaster.

They are known for telling "little white lies" and sometimes some big ones, because experience has taught them that bending the truth or avoiding it has been the surest way out of danger. This becomes habit-forming, part of the automatic-reaction pattern when dealing with anything threatening. Yet they tend to judge themselves without mercy, not a surprising practice since they have almost never felt the pleasure of reward. Such a tightly-wound individual is not always pleasant to be with because life is too serious a problem with never-ending complications.

To say the least, they have grave difficulty in intimate relationships, having felt the terror of abandonment on a regular basis, and obviously they cannot trust but instead have an insatiable need for approval and affirmation. Working with people on the job or in other cooperative efforts is difficult in that they have no idea what to expect from the other people; they must guess at what the reactions of others might be. Nonetheless, they try extremely hard to please and remain very loyal to relationships.

If ever they find a relationship that works, it is a treasure to be worried about and protected at all cost. However, some have managed to develop a "science" of knowing how to please even the most impossible people and will do so endlessly at great cost to their own personhood.

7 Abuse at School

Sexual Harrassment

Child abuse occurs in school with alarming frequency. Some 25 percent of females and 10 percent of males in grades eight through eleven have admitted to being sexually harassed by a teacher or other member of school faculty (Shakeshaft, 1995). Tamara Elaine Shulman (1995) writes,

> When a child is molested or sexually abused, his or her innocence has been unjustly stolen. Such a child is scarred for life once he or she has been violated by anyone, especially if that person is a teacher—a person who deserves a child's respect and trust.
>
> Unfortunately, teachers who molest children in schools are depriving them of their natural instincts to trust. Without trust, a student-teacher relationship is impossible. If a child puts his or her trust in a teacher, a bond is created. That bond is fragile, and if broken, it causes children to re-evaluate the trust they have already placed in other individuals they care about.

Elementary-age children, being in Erikson's industry versus inferiority stage, are trying to realize basic competencies, to compete, and to excel. But the true self is entering subordination according to my model, and the false self is gaining influence. The illusion of power is carrying the child through this mild confusion and motivating him to continue exploration of self.

Abuse at this stage increases the momentum of the takeover by the false self as critical messages are conveyed: "You cannot trust; your power is gone; look at what

Teacher did to you against your will; something wrong or bad in you caused this to happen." Further, even though the child will sense powerlessness, in conflict with his illusion of power, his or her illusion of power may be increased, for sexual abuse conveys to the child a long-lasting message that there is power in sex: power to control other people, even authorities.

Here is yet another reason that a girl, for example, may exhibit seemingly promiscuous behavior in adolescence and early adulthood: There is real power in sexuality, and this power comforts the haunting sense of helplessness.

Psychologist David Finkelhor (1986), an established authority on child abuse, has studied the results of schools that have instituted classes to teach children what sexual abuse is. He has found, in interviewing over 2000 school children, that children have a much easier time telling someone about being abused (no matter who the offender is) when they are in a supportive workshop environment. The feeling of safety in opening up is increased when the children hear stories of what others have been through.

Insult as Control

Far more common than sexual abuse in schools is the use of insult either in order to control students' behavior or as a means of venting frustration. Decades ago, teachers routinely paddled or whipped misbehaving children. Verbal putdowns and threats were not required. Today, there is a general, if not airtight, prohibition against corporal punishment of any kind in the classroom, and teachers are increasingly frustrated by not having a suitable way to control their students.

Greater creativity needs to be applied to the control of school children without either corporal or other punishment.

There are ways to apply discipline without damaging the child's image, especially when it is strongly emphasized that punishment and worth are not related. The message needs to be kept clear that certain behaviors have their own consequences and that the child has the power to control the behavior.

Recently I evaluated an 11-year-old black girl at her home, in the presence of her 10-year-old brother and loving, doting grandmother. Both children had been raised with a strong value system that included loving and respecting themselves and other people. Their experiences in school had been uneventful for the most part until the present school year.

The girl had been on a school bus loaded with other children, almost all of them black. The driver had returned the children from another location back to the school because of noisy behavior on the part of the group. When the bus arrived, the white principal boarded the bus and in anger called them all "niggers."

This girl had never heard that term used before in such a way, and she was not sure of its meaning, although she knew it was bad. She had thought that the word pertained to anyone who was irresponsible, lazy, or stupid. Only when she got home and talked to her grandmother did she discover that the word is what some white people call black people.

The interpretation was that she was a nigger, with every negative connotation. Her reaction was not rage, not defiance, not protest, but shame. She looked away as she related this incident, and there were tears in her eyes, but with the complete absence of any hostility toward the principal or anyone else.

Her brother added that he had been called the same name by the same principal twice, once when no-one knew that he had overheard the comment. His interpretation and his reaction were similar to his sister's.

The children's illusion of power, rightfully belonging to them at that developmental stage, had been stripped. What should have been a time of channeling their process of becoming was detoured to an acceptance of information that was completely false—a lie. The subordination of self was accelerated as the false self took on more solid identity based on the lie.

A 7-year-old boy was referred for evaluation regarding another type of school abuse: He had been taped to his classroom chair all day for weeks at a time and was forced at other times to face the wall all day long. The teacher had said the punishment was due to his not sitting still. These outrages had occurred when the child was a kindergarten student.

I found him to be lethargic and depressed, plus lacking in normal spontaneity and sense of play. He was overly obedient, complacent, still, and quiet. His predominant affect was shame. This small boy had received information about himself by a mother substitute: his teacher, whose job it is to nurture and encourage.

The child's knowledge level was grossly below his demonstrated intelligence. It was obvious that he had basically stopped learning. Since a previous, independent examination by a child psychiatrist had ruled out a learning disability, it could only be concluded that this arrest of his learning process was the result of abuse, in school. His pre-school teacher had related that before he entered kindergarten he was a keen and bright child, full of curiosity, loving to learn. But at age 7, he was not able to name all of his colors, was slow in naming those he could, was able to count only to 29, and was not able to name the usual geometric shapes.

If we were to look at this child's condition, both in terms of learning theory and behaviorism, it would be easily seen that his natural inclination to explore his environment had been extinguished through repeated punishment and through sensory deprivation. The child had given up.

Misdiagnosis of Behavior

In the school systems, one of the most far-reaching and deeply damaging forms of abuse is the misdiagnosis or non-diagnosis of children's learning or behavioral problems. There is a critical need to understand the *root cause* of a child's academic difficulties rather than performing only standardized tests and then assigning the child to a broad, general category such as SLD (slow learning disability), EH (emotional handicap), and ADHD (attention-deficit, hyperactivity disorder).

In addition, once the etiology of the problem is diagnosed, recommendations must be given so that the child can overcome (at least to some extent) any disability through a treatment plan specifically tailored to the needs of the individual. Such a plan should focus not only on limitations but on maximizing intact cognitive functions. There is little if any individualization in forming the child's IEP (individualized educational plan).

In the school systems I have dealt with, in Florida and South Carolina, there is little or no effort made to discover *why* a child has a difficulty. The "why" is covered over with a label.

An attorney I have worked with found it necessary to bring a lawsuit against the entire city in order to acquire a diagnosis and a treatment plan for his son. The school system insisted that these tasks had been accomplished. Their diagnosis was "anoxia," not a diagnosis at all but an event (oxygen deprivation). The diagnosis lies in what effect the anoxia had on the child's development. This is equivalent to a diagnosis of "football" when the condition is a broken arm.

In schools, as in the case with this child, students are almost never evaluated neuropsychologically. Brain damage, whether localized or global, is not considered. It is therefore impossible to determine which cognitive functions can be maximized and which can be somewhat improved, if possible.

In the case of emotionally handicapped children and adolescents, it has been my strong belief for 20 years that these disturbances are not "self contained" and free-standing in the manner of medical conditions. They do not rise up from nowhere. For one thing, a child is a "barometer" reflecting his life experiences at home. Therefore, without being intrusive, the family system and the home environment must be comprehended adequately. If, for a time, a child has performed well but then begins to exhibit difficulties, something in the child's life has changed. But this obvious fact is not addressed in any sufficient manner.

Millions more dollars are poured out on school systems every year as politicians make new promises to improve education. They seem to believe that if they improve buildings, construct more buildings, pressure teachers into advanced education, establish merit systems, etc., then the system will produce a better "product".

The major question to be addressed, instead of all of these palliative approaches, is not why teachers cannot teach, but why students cannot learn. Most of the answers lie at home, not within the school walls.

One seasoned psychologist I know applied as an educational psychologist in a particular school district. The senior psychologist met with him and made it clear that he would not want such a job. She said, "All we do is test and then assign to special-education classes. Test and assign, test and assign." The applicant looked elsewhere for employment.

An experienced middle-school teacher has found that both she and her colleagues have lost complete control of the classroom. She has found it impossible to teach in the usual way because of chaos ruling at all times: students fighting, yelling, throwing, running around, and other confusion. There is no way that she can make them behave. Her solution is to take her portable radio to work, and sit at her desk with earphones always on.

There are a few students in the room who are trying against these odds to acquire an education. When one of them approaches her desk, the teacher puts down the earphones and instructs, one individual at a time.

These eager students are being abused by the administration. Children who will not behave or accept discipline should not be allowed to attend school. The educational setting should be exclusively devoted to those students who are willing to learn-or at least willing not to interfere with the learning of others.

The vast majority of teachers are very capable of teaching well. They are not the problem. The crisis is that they are unable to do their jobs. The solution is not more money thrown at the problem but a resolve on the part of school administrators, law enforcement, and the legislature to change the school environment.

Three brothers were all independently told by their irresponsible principal that they were not "college material." Not coming from a wealthy family in a class-conscious school, the boys had been excluded by other students from the circles of influence where wealth, social standing, and academics were valued. They were relegated to the "lower" classes of friends not only by students but also by teachers who adhered to the school's class system.

Fortunately, each boy had sufficient sense of self to ignore his high-school experience. One is today the vice-president of a large banking conglomerate, the second is the youngest full partner on record in the world's largest accounting firm, and the third is a doctor.

Many adolescents, as well as younger children, however, are not as fortunate. They make an estimation of their intelligence, motivation, and general capacity based on the strong opinions of teachers, other school personnel, and classmates. Many make determinations as to their worth as people, again based on unreliable information which is, most tragically, the only information available.

In the middle-school and high-school years, abuse occurs at the hands of other students as they discover experimental identities in cliques and systematically exclude other children who do not meet the criteria for membership. At a time when the young person is searching for an identity that might work in society—that is, experimentally "becoming"—the peer group brandishes the weapon of exclusion. The peers can make a "leper" out of a child who doesn't fit their standards.

Again, this is an administrative challenge. Principals and counselors, as well as teachers, know about the cliques. They should be discouraged and replaced with efforts to build a school-wide identity. Clique members should be addressed individually and made to understand how damaging their groups are to those excluded from them. Members of such groups also cheat themselves, for they acquire a group identity rather than develop further as individuals.

The reality is, however, that if a child's clothes bear the wrong label, or if he misses a sudden style change, he can become a pariah. The same can happen if he is too heavy, too thin, or in any way not resembling the always changing criteria for acceptance. One boy attending an upscale prep school wore a jacket that had the exact look of being in style but had the "wrong" label. Other students ripped the jacket off his back and tore it to shreds.

Covering It Up

There is a great deal of cover-up in the operation of schools. When children are attacked by other students repeatedly, the administration, plus the teachers obeying the administration, will deny that such incidents are occurring. The same lawyer I spoke of earlier found it necessary to sue the system for his child's protection. Security officers, on duty always, are required to report violence, but they do not always comply because the main part of their jobs is to prevent the violence from occurring. An incident is a "black mark" against the officer and the administration.

Ideally, school-district superintendents and school principals should hold the primary accountability for all of the problems discussed above. Unfortunately, the administrative education and training for such jobs is unlike those in industry. Qualifications are severely lacking.

Many are promoted school teachers who have never managed any group other than a classroom. In one school district in Florida, a retired Navy officer was hired as superintendent of an enormous system, even though he knew no more about education than the students and had never managed any organization except for his own Naval command.

8 Neglect and Rejection

Researching Neglect

This section relies heavily on the pioneering and masterful work of Martha Farrell Erickson and Byron Egeland (1996), researchers in the Minnesota Mother-Child Interaction

Their research project, begun in 1975, traces the development of children identified before birth as being at high risk for neglect. The key factors used to classify the nearly 300 children as being at risk for poor developmental outcomes were poverty; early age of mother (mean, 20); low maternal education; marital instability or absence of marriage (67 percent); and stressful life circumstances. The authors write,

> While the bruises and scars of physical abuse are more readily apparent, the quiet assault of neglect often does at least as much damage to its young victims... and sometimes neglect just slowly and persistently eats away at the child's spirit until she has little will to connect with others or explore the world...

Out of the total sample of 267 children, 44 were physically abused, neglected, abandoned, or otherwise mistreated during the first two years of life. Of these, 24 were identified as neglected: Their parent(s) did not adequately provide for physical needs, the home environment was often unsafe, and the children were not adequately supervised.

Nineteen mothers were identified as "psychologically unavailable," meaning unresponsive to their children, failing to provide nurturance, comfort, positive responses to children's efforts at gaining attention, and not interacting with or showing interest in their child.

At 42 months, the neglected children were rated low on self-esteem and self-assertion, as well as ego control, flexibility, and creativity. They were withdrawn, easily frustrated, and lacking in persistence and enthusiasm, the authors report.

The neglected children had difficulty coping as they went through preschool. They were more dependent than children in the control group; scored lower in learning skills; and were developmentally delayed. In early elementary school, the children displayed severe problems in a number of areas, including attentiveness, involvement, self-reliance and creativity. They were impatient, disrespectful, anxious about school work, and likely to make irrelevant responses in the schoolroom. They were seen as both aggressive/acting out or as passive/withdrawn.

Further, the neglected children showed poor emotional health, lack of social competence, and increased attention-seeking. They had extreme difficulty adjusting to kindergarten. By 6th grade, all had been referred for special help, and 58 percent had been retained in their first two years of school.

"The failure of a child's caretaker to provide the necessary emotional responsiveness has devastating consequences on the early development of the child... Most disturbing was the sharp increase in the number of anxiously attached children from the 12 to 19-month assessment. Whereas at 12 months, 44 percent of the children in the psychologically unavailable group were anxiously attached, by 18 months, none of the children in this group was securely attached.

Clearly, the failure to nurture the infant emotionally resulted in the infant's resorting to a coping style that was a pattern of avoiding emotional contact, as if "I'm going to reject her before she can reject me again."

The authors state that by 54 months, factors such as aggressiveness, noncompliance, defiance, and disrespect were prevalent. They caused class disturbances and were described as unpopular, nervous and overactive. The problems continued in sixth grade, and the children were described by teachers as withdrawn, unpopular, inattentive, and low in achievement.

> Some investigators would disagree with our findings and argue that some children are not adversely affected by maltreatment. The reason some investigators have failed to find effects for all maltreated children is that they assessed development at one point in time rather than longitudinally, and assessed a narrow band of functioning (e.g., anger) rather than comprehensive assessments based on the salient developmental issues of a particular age.
>
> We found different patterns of maladaption at different ages. Many of our neglected children had difficulty coping in school, some lacked competence, some were angry, and some had low IQs. The patterns of maladaption were not identical; however, all showed ill effects in some area of development, and by the time they were of school age the effects were severe."

Using my own terms, these children were robbed of their right to express and explore their true selves through social interaction, mainly with Mother. Their false self was hastened in its arrival due to the nature of the conclusions a child draws about himself when ignored: "I don't exist. I don't count." They were denied the opportunity for their imaginary becoming, because no efforts paid off; and their taste of power was obliterated.

Rejection

While neglect is certainly a form of rejection, there are some children who are raised in fierce, open, and active discarding by a parent. Here, there is no subtlety. Some adults have never gotten over the vivid image of a father's icy stare signifying hateful contempt for the very personhood of the child. This kind of clear and total rejection is never fully overcome but can be carried, scars and all, if the true self is developed sufficiently through intensive, insight-oriented therapy aimed at throwing off the lies communicated during childhood.

In one of the most extreme cases I have treated, a widower with a 5-year-old son, Luke, married a woman who had not been married before and had no children of her own. From the very start, she became irritated by almost everything the boy did or said, even though the child had a very gentle and sweet personality and was very obedient. This little one, having his real mother's death still weighing on him, endured constant nagging and direct verbal abuse by his stepmother.

With each new child born to the couple, the rejection of Luke became worse. Stepmother eventually stopped pretending, quit hiding her hostility, even when visitors were present in the home. In time, anyone could see that she blatantly "had it in" for the boy. By the time he reached his teens, he tried to stay away from home as much as possible.

A very bright child, he lost all motivation; became a substandard student; gave up the career dreams and fantasies of his earlier childhood; and began to settle for existence rather than life. Luke was convinced that he deserved nothing. Even his father had given up any emotional support and gave all of his attention to the later children, those he shared with his wife. One day, when she was sure the boy would be away, the stepmother took everybody else to the photographic studio for a family portrait.

It happened that one night, as a young adult, this same victim, Luke, had managed to spend some time with his father, and the two had gotten very drunk. He used the occasion to ask the question that had plagued him all of his life: "Why did you never love me?" The father looked at him and said nothing as the son implored him again and again to answer. No answer ever came-not that night, not ever.

The son could not adjust to this horrible reality.

Processing the information, grieving, and moving on would be impossible until the condition made some kind of sense. He performed his own therapy by never giving up his search for a cause. Then, one day, through a distant family member, he received his answer: The man he thought was his father all of his life was not. He further learned that his deceased mother had been extremely promiscuous all during the marriage, and any one of a long list of men could be his real father.

Compared to the rejection issue, the identity of his biological father did not matter very much. Luke had solved his problem, for now there was an explanation. From the very instant of his discovery, he was relieved. Little grieving was necessary, because he had indeed mourned the issue all of his life. Now he knew the problem was not with himself. He became somewhat empowered, and very soon began the work of exploring who he really was, apart from being anyone's son. Very essential to him was a strong spirituality that enabled him to put the matter largely to rest by concluding that he was on Earth because his heavenly Father willed that he be here, and further, that there was an excellent purpose for his life.

Some children experience the brunt of rejection even when they are, in fact, loved. There are many parents who are quite able to love but not able to demonstrate it because of their own deficiencies in the way they were raised. A parent who has missed a warm, accepting, and openly affectionate relationship with his own parent can be disabled in what would be normal parent-child interaction. But such unfortunates are not aware of the deficiency because most people feel that what occurred in their families of origin was normal. Thus this "partial parenting," without intervention, will be passed on from one generation to another and will tend to produce "robotized" adults.

The best example I have ever witnessed of a father-son relationship was that of our neighbors across the street in the suburbs of Philadelphia. The time was long before I had even begun to study psychology, so I was concerned at all the affection that Tom showed for his son, Tommy, then about 9 or 10. Tom often picked him up without warning and kissed him on the cheek, pull him up on his lap, and stood with his arm around the boy, all to the point where I thought he would make his son into a "sissy". But I never commented on my opinion. In fact, Tom and I became very close friends.

As the years went by, I saw Tommy becoming more and more masculine, with the affection between father and son remaining very much in force. One night, when the boy was about 14, I was seated in their very large living room when Tommy came down the stairs. He looked around the room, saw several vacant seats, walked straight over to his father and sat down on his lap, as though that was his usual seat. Tom had been talking at the time, but never missed a word as he finished what he was saying.

Tommy became a man in the fullest sense, because Tom had passed on his own masculinity to the boy every time he delivered affection. The child's "welcome to manhood" had always been fully extended.

Rejection is however the strong message children receive when they are blamed for their parents' marriage problems. Many are told that "If it weren't for you kids, your father and I would never fight." Children, of course, take this information at face value and internalize it as valid. They may not realize how absurd the claim was until they become married and experience the reality that children are not the cause of marriage problems. In fact, and tragically, some children are born with the assignment of saving their parents' hopeless marriage in a last-ditch effort before divorce.

A child can suffer rejection because he reminds Mother (or Father) of herself, when Mother is furious with herself or seems to hate herself. The child might, alternatively, trigger memories of a hated or feared relative. At a time when the child is just being himself, he can receive a glare or a shout of correction for no apparent reason. Such children might actually be told directly, "You're just like your Aunt Ruth," or something similar. Again, the child absorbs the comment as fact about himself.

Too often, little girls are molested by their fathers, but more often by stepfathers. Many a mother will blame the child in order to preserve a positive regard for her mate. Mother has probably married such a man due to her own history. Since the child innately already believes that the atrocity is her fault, Mother's not believing her or, worse, blaming her casts in concrete the child's conclusion that she is herself bad.

Typically, the child will be so obsessed with the subject of her own sexuality that she will experiment lavishly in adolescence, as previously discussed. She will think sexually, feel sexual, and act sexual in the misdirection that her process of becoming has taken. Her taste of power and her illusion of power will be sexually based.

It is therefore no wonder that she will give off enough sexual energy to attract one or more predators. Thus, it is typical for molested little girls to be raped later in life. The rape obviously drives the foundation even deeper that her whole being consists of sexuality; that is, bad sexuality. Because she is bad, she is unworthy of decent companionship and is thus amenable to forming a partnership with an abusive male. In her mind, she deserves no better. When the abuse of that first significant relationship becomes intolerable, she will seek another partner, only to find him more abusive than the first.

Some girls will make a career out of sex as a dancer or a prostitute, with each dance or each "trick" confirming still further her sexual being and her badness. Many turn to drugs or alcohol, and most get arrested repeatedly, with the arrests by now not mattering because this condemnation by society fits well with the fully developed false self. Any illusion of power is long gone, except for sexual power, but that power is bad. All hope for "becoming" has long been given up.

It also happens in the opposite reaction too: the girl who rejects all sexuality, and disguises herself as physically unattractive.

The worst example of rejection that has come to my attention is addressed by M. Scott Peck (1983). He cites a case study in which the parents of a boy who had committed suicide by shooting himself gave the same gun to their other son as a Christmas gift. In his best-selling book, *People of the Lie,* he establishes the reality of literal evil in human beings. Among the characteristics of such people are several that have been confirmed over and over in my practice: 1) Evil people present an air-tight facade of being good; 2) they never admit being wrong, and 3) the people closest to them suffer major emotional damage.

An example is the mother described earlier who told her anorexic daughter that if the girl could get over it, "I can die in peace." While it would be comforting to think that it is both natural and universal for parents to love their children, experience dictates otherwise. There are some parents who hate their children, and the ones most suspect are those who try to possess their offspring for their own purposes, forever.

<table>
<tr><td>**9**</td><td># Domestic
Abuse</td><td></td></tr>
</table>

Recently I addressed a county mental health association in a small South Carolina town. I began with the same startling sentence I had used on other occasions: "Domestic violence begins at 4." The doctors and nurses, though silent, were indeed puzzled as I scanned their faces. Because every child blames herself for the abuse or neglect she has suffered, the "my fault" message, deeply internalized, navigates the individual throughout life. Abuse, once begun, takes on a life of its own and finds people and occasions throughout life to multiply itself.

The abused little girl becomes the abused adolescent, who becomes an abused adult. Just as water seeks its own level, so an abused person seeks relationships and a lifestyle that are no better than what she believes she deserves.

Abusive men seem to have an uncanny intuition in being able to identify a girl or woman they can victimize. They can spot her a block away. Once they have their claws into her, they never let go. Even when a domestic violence victim gathers enough strength and support in a shelter to leave her present captor, she is not rid of him, because he follows, he stalks, and he torments from a distance in any way he can.

The Mennonite Domestic Violence Task Force (Lehman, 1996) has assembled 16 traits of an abuser that my own patients have studied in amazement. They are incredulous at the fact that their own tormentor fits this description so closely. Items 17 on are derived from my own observations through treating abused women.

Signs of the Abuser

1. He is jealous and tries to "own" his partner.

2. He blames others for his faults.

3. He blames circumstances for his difficulties.

4. He demonstrates unpredictable behavior.

5. He belittles his partner verbally and tries to convince her she's crazy.

6. He cannot control his anger.

7. He always asks for another chance.

8. He promises and swears to change.

9. He may have been abused as a child or witnessed his father bully his mother.

10. He plays on his partner's guilt. ("If only you loved me, you would...")

11. His behavior often worsens when he uses alcohol or drugs.

12. He is closed-minded. His way is the only way.

13. He may seem charming and gentle to non-family members and the outside world.

14. He dislikes women, believes that a "woman's place is in the home," and that men have a right to possess women.

15. He may abuse his (or her) children by insult, intimidation, yelling, threatening, or actual violence.

16. He either refuses treatment, saying "You're the problem," or accepts treatment but plays games with the therapist.

17. He expects his partner to pay her own way financially.

18. He does not believe his partner when he asks where she's been.

19. He forces her into sex and other behaviors that she does not want.

20. He acts as though all income is his.

21. He threatens suicide or to kill her if she tries to leave.

22. He prevents her from making friends and/or engaging with her family.

23. He belittles her achievements and sabotages her accomplishments by insult.

24. He convinces her that he is doing her a favor by keeping her.

25. He either threatens violence or carries it out or both.

26. He forbids her to make decisions on her own.

27. He repeatedly hammers away at her incompetence.

28. He belittles her friends and/or family.

29. He is unpredictable and undependable as a provider, often putting all responsibility for income on his partner.

30. He continues to stalk, harass, threaten, and frighten her in cunning ways, even when an injunction for protection has been issued.

Regarding item 9, in my own experience men who have been abused as children are less likely, not more, to abuse women. While some studies tend to uphold item 9, they are based on men who are known abusers and who blame the fact on their childhood. Blaming others is a chief characteristic of an abuser. People who have been abused, whether male or female, tend to be compassionate, sensitive, and perceptive people.

Item 30, referring to a court-ordered injunction, bears special mention because police departments generally do not enforce such injunctions and often do not even serve them. In my work with an attorney in a major southern city, it was necessary to sue the sheriff's office in order to have an injunction served and enforced. The attorney and I underwent threats and intimidation by the police while the lawsuit was underway. The attorney's home was broken into, and his 90-year-old grandmother was threatened.

In every state, an injunction for protection is a court order, and it is the law for police to enforce the order.

However, at this writing, many police departments were permitted to make their own decision as to whether to serve such an injunction or not. It was left to the discretion of the individual police officer what action to take, if any.

Domestic violence shelters routinely walk the victim through the process of obtaining an injunction, with the result being false security. They are not warned that the injunction may further enrage the abuser and place the victim in further, immediate danger.

A major exception is the State of Massachusetts, which has revamped its traditional ways of responding to domestic abuse. (AOL News Bulletin, February, 1999). Whenever a police officer has reason to believe that a person has been abused, or is in danger of being abused, the officer must use all reasonable means to prevent further abuse. By law, the officer is required to remain on the scene until there is no longer a threat of danger; assist the abused person in obtaining medical treatment; and help the victim get to a safe place. The officer must give the abused a notice of his or her rights and, if necessary, facilitate an emergency judicial response system now in place.

The officer is required to arrest any person when probable cause indicates that a domestic abuse prevention order has been violated.

These changes have come about at a time when wives have remained the most frequent victims of family murders for at least six years at this writing (U.S. Dept. Justice, 1994), and the incidents of horror continue to rise. A study of more that 8,000 homicides in large urban counties, the Bureau of Justice Statistics reported that a male is the assailant in about two-thirds of family murders. According to the study, 56 percent of the murderers had been previously convicted of other offenses.

Only a woman programmed all her life would marry such a man.

Abuse against women should be treated as a global health problem, according to a sweeping new report that states at least one of every three women has been beaten, raped, or somehow mistreated. The Associated Press (1999), reporting on a newly released study conducted by the Johns Hopkins School of Public Health and the Center for Health and Gender Equity, says the study is the first to take a close look worldwide at the subject. The report, "Ending Violence Against Women" (Heise, 1999), said that abused women suffer from depression and physical problems, and their children are more likely to be stillborn or die in infancy.

"Most of this stuff has never seen the light of day," said co-author Lori Heise, who visited some 20 countries during the past decade to collect data from some 2,000 other studies of domestic violence. Between 22 and 70 percent of the women interviewed had never before told anyone about the abuse they had suffered. Beyond recent, visible injuries, abuse has now been linked to gastrointestinal disorders and chronic pain syndrome, as well as gynecological problems, complicated pregnancies, and substance abuse.

The report asserts that the health-care system is the only institution that interacts with nearly all women during their lives, and that health professionals are in a unique position to identify and assist victims. "I see the health care setting as an opportunity," Heise states, but "...right now it's an opportunity lost."

Speaking to the Associated Press, Dr. John Nelson, a spokesman for the American Medical Association, said that a poll commissioned by the organization found that abused women would rather speak to their physician than to anyone else.

Violence against women should be treated as a health issue, not just a legal matter, the report asserts. In Nicaragua, children of abused women were six times more likely to die before age 5, and women in India who had been beaten were more likely than others to face miscarriages, stillbirths, or infant deaths, Heise reports.

Why Women Stay

Why do women, especially in America, put up with these outrages? The chief reason is obedience to the messages of childhood, that they deserve no better. Many people find it difficult to believe, but the greater the abuse, the greater is the obedience factor.

A very strange phenomenon occurred at the end of World War II. When the allied troops came to free the prisoners of war, when the fences were down and the captors in custody, some prisoners refused to leave the camp. They would huddle and resist being moved. It was found that the captors who had been most cruel, most sadistic, and most forceful had won the greatest loyalty of their captives. Thus, there is this dependable equation, which I have seen in hundreds of abused women: the greater the abuse, the greater the obedience.

It is my premise that the normal way for both children and adults to react to abuse is to obey the message it conveys. Herein lies the reason that victims are so resistant to change, even when competent therapy is provided. To disobey the message of the tormentor is akin to being a traitor.

Another factor is that terrifying abusers live as phantoms in the minds of their victims. Many an adult, woman or man, feels that the original abuser, and often the present abuser, is "living in their head." This almost magical presence living on in the mind of a victim is sometimes so acutely felt that it has a voice of its own that can be confused as a hallucination. The communication is always negative and condemning and is continuously repeating the original message that "you are no good; you are not a real person; you dare not try to do better."

The difference between this kind of "voice" and hallucinations is that the former is more in line with a constant flashback, or memory so vivid that the abuser can almost be heard; however, the victim knows that the voice is a reliving experience. Hallucinations, as they occur in schizophrenia, are believed by the patient to be as real as any other reality.

The child, or "true self," as I name it, can be thought of as having an impermeable layer of protection around it. Such might also be thought of as a boundary, or a wall, enclosing the self. The abuser, by attacking the personhood of his victim, continuously assaults this barrier until at last he breaks all the way through and "sets up residence" inside.

Prisoners of war experience the same sensation through brainwashing. The barrier of the self is weakened by the infliction of excruciating pain that continues beyond endurance. Combined with sleep and food deprivation, the pain is applied with dehumanizing insults, in some way implanting the same message, no matter what words are used: "You are nobody."

The brainwashing is complete when the tormentor has broken through and has begun to live inside the mind of the victim. This is the nature and the power of child abuse. It is brainwashing of the first magnitude, accomplished with greater ease because the subject is a child, without power. When done effectively, brainwashing conditions the victim to accept the role of captive permanently. Hence, in domestic violence, we do not have a new occurrence of a destructive relationship resulting from a poor choice or a mistake that anyone could make. We have a continuation of the same earlier brainwashing with one abuser continuing where the other left off.

Minor reasons that battered, insulted, overly controlled, or humiliated women do not leave include the following:

- Hope that the partner will change.
- Partially believing that trying harder will make a difference.
- Fear of what the partner may do in retaliation (a well-grounded fear, implying that the victim needs protection).
- Not knowing what to do about the children.
- Lack of money.

- Having no place to go.
- Not knowing whom to call.
- Thinking that nothing can be done.
- Fear of living alone, without support.
- Thinking the problem isn't that bad, after all.
- Feeling the police and the courts won't help enough or fast enough (true in many cities).
- Religious and moral convictions.
- Fear of the unknown.

A critical item to be added to the above list is that many women are not conscious of the fact that they are in an abusive relationship. Their life experience, with the internalized messages that define their self image, prevents them from recognizing how preposterous their situation is. For this reason I have developed the checklist below.

This inventory (see p. 105), which has been administered to approximately 100 women known to have been abused by their partners, has yielded the consistent response: "I didn't know I was being abused until I took the test. I thought my relationship was normal but just had some problems."

Therefore, the intent is to help victims realize that they are in an abusive relationship. The inventory is for use by counselors, psychologists, psychiatrists, social workers, clergy, lawyers, physicians, police, child protection workers, and others, either to determine the likelihood of abuse or to convince the victim that she is indeed being abused, and thus break through the brainwashing described above.

It is my strong assertion that this checklist or one like it should be in the hands of all of the following, for very frequent usage:

- Emergency departments
- Rape crisis centers
- Domestic abuse shelters

- Courthouses—the department where women file injunctions for protection (usually under the State Attorney's office)
- Community mental health centers
- Drug and alcohol treatment centers
- Psychiatric hospitals and hospital departments of psychiatry
- City offices of victim services
- Women's advocacy groups
- Police departments
- Physicians' offices

Consequences of Staying

As they continue their subsistence in this type of prison environment, they face any of the following, as a consequence of staying:

- Further injury or death
- Depression
- Suicidal tendencies
- Increasing helplessness (illusion of powerlessness)
- Shutdown of everyday functioning
- Acute and chronic anxiety, often with panic attacks and/or agoraphobia
- Economic disaster
- Severe symptoms in children
- Social isolation
- Post-traumatic stress disorder (discussed at length later)

Because social isolation is a consequence, the woman is usually without a good enough friend to help with a rescue operation; that is, to help her leave and provide what is necessary for housing, child care, and all the other requirements for breaking the cycle. As a result, many cities have established programs to perform these life-saving functions.

A problem with most programs is that they are used heavily by the economically and culturally deprived. Middle-class women are subjected to a culture shock when suddenly thrust into a milieu that is foreign to them. These shelters tend to have a "ghetto" atmosphere, and in some the living conditions are deplorable.

These domestic violence projects usually assist victims in filing restraining orders against their oppressors. The victims feel somewhat comforted by such a court injunction until they find out that the piece of paper is worthless, as discussed previously. The victims receive group therapy by paraprofessionals and volunteers with an anti-male slant. Upper-level mental-health professionals, such as psychologists and psychiatrists, are rarely associated with these havens except perhaps on a consulting basis. Few of these consultants, however, are familiar with the treatment of emotional trauma or any of the roots of domestic violence.

I mean no less than to say that many of these facilities are in the "Dark Ages" regarding what a victim needs. But these organizations, for the most part, are deeply entrenched in the community and not open to change nor the application of effective treatment by well-qualified professionals. They have staked out their territory, and they are not about to allow outsiders within their borders.

My attorney-friend, of whom I spoke earlier, joined me at a meeting of a domestic-violence task force. When he pointed at that injunctions were neither being served nor enforced, he was branded as a trouble-maker and forbidden to come back. I was told that I could return if I did not interfere but to "keep that lawyer away from here."

A "model" facility, according to my view, would be headed by a full-time social worker or psychologist who has thoroughly studied child abuse, emotional trauma, and the treatment of both. As discussed later, the treatment of domestic violence is the treatment of child abuse for the most part, and it is always the treatment of emotional trauma, quite often post-traumatic stress disorder. This director would also have enough training in neuropsychology to diagnose traumatic brain injuries. In addition, an attorney with training and experience in abuse would be retained on a contract, on-call basis.

It is common knowledge that more than one-third of women who visit emergency departments are there for on-going abuse and that up to two-thirds of these victims are beaten while pregnant. Yet, the abuse is rarely reported. Further, the patients are "patched up" and released to return to their battleground.

Even though blows to the head and face cause most visible injuries, the likelihood of brain damage is not explored except in rare cases, and then only by electronic imaging. These diagnostic tools, such as MRIs, miss most types of brain damage, as do routine neurological examinations. The majority of brain injuries are detectable only through neuropsychological testing, which detect cognitive deficiencies. Hospitals, however, generally shun psychologists, so that they are rarely on staff to perform such evaluations, and they are not included as a referral source. Psychiatrists receive the referrals, if any are made, and they, in turn, are not familiar with neuropsychological diagnostics or else prefer not to resort to the expertise of a psychologist.

There are many exceptions to the exclusion of psychologists by hospitals, but the two professions of psychiatry and psychology do not generally work conjointly as logic would dictate. As a result, most of the head injuries occurring as a result of child and/or domestic abuse are not detected.

Brain Damage Symptoms

Contrary to fact, the myth remains that head injuries are caused only by an impact to some part of the head. Both psychologists and psychiatrists, when examining victims, should inquire about falls, unconsciousness, whiplash-type incidents, and anoxic events, to name only a few causes. Attorneys as well should ask these questions and many more. The following are not always symptoms of brain injury, but they can be, and a combination certainly warrants further procedures for a useful diagnosis:

- Memory loss
- Slowed thinking
- Pauses during questioning
- Vision or hearing changes, including double vision and tinnitus
- Dizziness
- Loss of balance
- Difficulty communicating
- Headaches
- Misjudging distances
- Trouble understanding verbal communication
- Tremors, seizures, spasms
- Confusion
- Confabulation (making up stories)
- Trouble performing routine tasks
- Unusual gait
- Numbness or tingling, any part of body
- Decreased initiative
- Personality change
- Denial of an evident mental problem
- Agitation
- Anxiety and/or depression without a history of same
- Impulsiveness
- Odd movements or behaviors
- Nightmares
- Social withdrawal
- Explosive rage (especially without recall)
- Chronic fatigue
- Self-centeredness
- Over-reaction to sudden noises or movements
- Loss of former interests

A recent patient of mine. Maggie, received such massive brain damage in a beating by her partner that she was not expected to live. She remained unconscious on life support for weeks. When she resumed consciousness, she was blind in one eye, she had lost her ability to speak, and her emotional control was severely affected. She would laugh at every question she was asked.

The mother of four children, Maggie had been a vibrant, energetic worker at her job, and was well-liked due to her delightful personality. Her injuries disabled her to the extent that she could not care for her children, so she and her children took up residence with her mother, who had severely abused her verbally throughout her life and who proceeded to scream at the children constantly. I had attempted to treat her at home, but the grandmother's screaming made this impossible. It was necessary to arrange special transportation so that she could come to my office.

Maggie remained in love with her batterer, and for her own safety had to be watched constantly so that she would not sneak back to see him. He had received a sentence of only six months in jail, but served only half of that.

An ideal shelter would care for both the mother and her children, but certainly not in an "institutional" environment as is mostly the case. The ambiance would be resort-like and would provide ample privacy. Instead of making the victims prepare their own meals and clean their own quarters, they would be "pampered" as guests who had earned the right to "royal" treatment through what they had suffered.

A family physician, a pediatrician, and a gynecologist would be on-call, contractually. Instead of riding in a van to a clinic, they would receive their medical care on-site. There would be a play area for children, well supervised by gentle staff. There might be an exercise room, but certainly a very pleasant social area, attractively and comfortably furnished. Each individual room would have its own bath and be equipped with TV, plush carpet, and other amenities.

One might say that the expense would be prohibitive. However, that is not the case, as professional fees would be covered by third-party payers, such as Medicaid, private insurance, or grant funding. The facility itself could be constructed with the help of an allocation of the city or County budget, or perhaps through private or corporate grants.

Specialized individual and group treatment would be available on a daily basis, including weekends, but attendance would be optional when first admitted. A full-time nurse who understands the issues and is perhaps a survivor would be a key staff member.

In brief, any connotation of punishment, "sentencing" or forced confinement must be completely reversed because, after all, the victim believes that she deserves punishment. That mindset is one of the first that must be countered.

Domestic Violence Inventory

1. Are you afraid of your partner?
2. Do you feel as though you have to "walk on egg-shells" to keep your partner from getting grouchy?
3. Has your partner ever hit, slapped, or punched you?
4. Do you feel you deserve to be punished?
5. Do you ever have the feeling you've done something wrong but you don't know what it is?
6. Have you lost respect or love for your partner?
7. Are you ever afraid your partner will hurt the children?
8. Have you ever daydreamed of killing or disabling your partner?
9. Is your partner good to you most of the time but suddenly gets scary?
10. Are the children afraid of your partner?
11. Does your partner ever tell you you're crazy?
12. Has your partner ever threatened to hurt you?
13. Do you ever fear you may be seriously hurt by your partner?
14. Has your partner ever threatened to commit suicide?
15. Has anybody warned you to get out of the relationship?
16. Were you abused or neglected as a child?
17. Has your partner forced you to do things you don't want to do?
18. If you say "no" to your partner, is there danger?
19. Have you lost any friends due to your partner?
20. Does your partner have to approve where you go and when?
21. Have you lost a job because of your partner?
22. Does your partner stop you from doing things you want to do?

23. Does your partner doubt your word; that is, not believe you?
24. Do you feel emotionally numb?
25. Are you afraid to tell anyone what's really going on?
26. Have you ever wanted to call the police or someone else for protection?
27. Do you ever feel hopeless about your situation?
28. Have you ever thought about running away?
29. Does your partner change when using alcohol or drugs?
30. Are you forced into sex when you're not willing?
31. Do you feel like your partner's personal possession?
32. Have you ever been in a violent or controlling relationship before?
33. Was there bad fighting in the family you grew up in?
34. Are you a grown child of an alcohol or drug abuser?

Only a few positive answers to the above questions, perhaps only one, are required as an indication of possible seriousness. Contrary to the belief of the victim, most women do not live this way, and would not continue to tolerate any of the outright offenses included above. But victims tend to stay in their captivity, mainly due to obedience, as stated, to the early childhood messages.

10 A Man's Account

Compared to domestic violence against women, the offense applied to men is rare but yet not absent. Male victims of domestic abuse are rarely attacked physically; instead, they are assaulted verbally and mentally in the partnership. In my practice I have treated both men and women, although in separate groups. Because the same dynamics apply for men; that is, child abuse leading to later abuse, it is worth devoting this account of one single case, because it is indeed an excellent example of the principles so far discussed.

At age 7, David believed that his father wanted him dead. Although he knows today that his father did love him, that terrible beating, with the dog-training weapon described earlier, caused him to become terrified in his father's presence from that day on.

Before, when he was younger, David was always excited to see his dad come home. He used to watch for him to appear up at the end of the block and run to go meet him. He would get a great big welcome from Dad, and it was the best part of the boy's day.

Sometime after the beating, while still in elementary school, David came to believe in God. But that only made things worse, because now there was someone even bigger and more powerful to keep at bay. So in order to avoid His wrath, the boy stopped whatever he was doing many times during the day and knelt down, then bent all the way forward to kiss the ground. This bizarre act became a "magical" way of keeping God from attacking him or his mother. He dared not stop the ritual, no matter how much the other children laughed at him. It was better to undergo complete humiliation many times every day than to take a chance. David had no imaginary power of his own; instead, the ritual held the power. He cannot remember how long that behavior continued, but he estimates more than a year.

He did not have any real interest in girls until he was 15. Even then, he preferred being with his friends, the guys he would explore the sewers with, go camping with, and watch late-night horror shows with. They were kids who did not fit in with the cliques at school. They were "in-betweeners": very intelligent but interested in nothing, fully capable of academic excellence but not considering college preparation something that would be natural for them. They simply existed.

One day, in 10th grade, there was a girl with a very pretty face sitting across the table from David in their classroom. He was moved to speak to her, and to his astonishment, she spoke back in a warm, encouraging way. After a few dates, a problem arose. She said that she did not want to be with somebody with only a "D" average and on the verge of failing algebra. Delores was an honor-roll student. So he knew he had to start trying, even though he did not really believe that he could do any better.

As they continued to date, Delores seemed to build David's experimental self. She gradually, over many conversations, started to make him think that he was intelligent and even had a special mission in life-perhaps being a pastor or something (even though she made it plain that she would never marry a pastor).

Delores seemed to have serious problems with her parents and sisters. As she and David talked and caressed intimately, time after time, over the next two years or so, she made him think he was helping her. (Of course, he was not, because he was a child himself). But to him, his experimental power became laced with a sense of value. It was also very clear to him how much Delores needed him as well. The process led to mutual dependence, even though David felt the price was too high. In other words, she demanded all of his time and all of his attention. He was no longer "allowed" to be with any other friend. She, on the contrary, had complete freedom to be with anyone she wished, whenever she wished.

David recalls one time in the summer when Delores went with her family to the seashore and said he couldn't visit her there because she was going to try dating some other people. He was unaware then, but this condition had been set as a ploy to "pull him in deeper." He did not know that he was about to become possessed by her.

A merger had occurred, in David's mind, through plentiful sexual activity, not including intercourse. He had begun to feel part of her, and to have her go away into someone else's arms rocked him to his already shaky foundations. He stayed in his bedroom the whole time she was away and suffered agony beyond anything he has been able to put into words. He did not understand what was happening to him, and certainly could not explain it. All he knew was that he was living in both anguish and terror.

He says had that trial lasted much longer, he would surely have died. He had fantasies of being the lead character in the movie, "The King and I," who wasted down to his last breath. He still cries when he sees that movie.

Delores, of course, did come back, and was more demanding of his time and emotional energy than ever. Once, when David resisted one of her manipulations, she broke into violence and started hitting him with her little fists. Certainly she did not hurt him physically; on the contrary he came to a moment of lucidity. He became almost empowered enough to break the relationship, but he caved in when she came to his house hysterically begging him to take her back.

David managed to go to college in a distant city, with the heavy assistance of his parents, both of whom wanted to get Delores out of their son's life. He was happier there than he had ever been. But about halfway through the second semester of his freshman year, she employed the "seashore" scam and informed him that she was planning to date other people. Her daily letters had given hints of her attraction to other young men, although they were packed with expressions of passionate love for him. The double messages kept him constantly off-balance. Finally, he decided to transfer to the college she attended. Her strategy had worked perfectly.

They were married in their junior year. David, fed up with the mixed communications, insisted that they would either marry or break up for good. Actually, they did both. When David returned from work the very day after their brief honeymoon, he found that she had slammed a window on her hand repeatedly and had burned her arm with matches. She had also been sitting at the top of the fire escape and said she was debating whether or not to jump off.

She never did.

For the next 13 years, without a break, she kept David believing that she was suicidal. Of course, it became his job to make sure she did not kill herself. The impossibility of his assignment, combined with his concern for her and the absolute unpredictability of each day's events, constantly sabotaged his adopted self.

David was forced to go to work every day without knowing whether he would find his wife alive when he returned. When he came in the door each night, he had to search for her and often find her in a closet refusing to talk. Sometimes he would succeed in getting her out of the closet, and sometimes he would not. When he did, she would parade around either topless or completely nude and then become furious when he wanted to touch her. The only time they had sex was when she decided she wanted to have a child. Then, when she did not get pregnant immediately, she became more "suicidal."

He took her to a psychologist, then a psychiatrist, then another psychiatrist, and in the 13th year a family therapist. The last course of therapy led to her becoming addicted to both alcohol and prescription drugs, and the "therapy" climaxed with her running away carrying a stash of pills, alcohol, and an antique pistol David's father had given him. After that event, the therapist refused to see her anymore.

It was just as well, because Delores had never talked—not at all—with any of the doctors she had seen.

In all, David had committed her to lock-up psychiatric facilities four times, once with the assistance of her own
mother. It was either commit her or allow the chance that
she might carry through her suicide threat. Only recently
has David, now a middle-aged man, realized that his wife
had numerous opportunities to kill herself but never did.
She killed David, at least his adopted self.

In this 13-year nightmare, David discovered a friend,
not in the form of a person, because he was permitted no
friends, but in the form of alcohol. He had always enjoyed
his drink at lunch and his martinis before dinner, all part
of normal living according the way he had been raised. But
about two years into the marriage, he found that a morning drink, before he left for work made it so much easier to
leave. He also discovered that the same procedure, before
coming back at night, greatly dulled the experience of
hunting for his wife.

He had long ago given up on God and the church people he had known. Neither God nor the people ever showed
up to help him, or even called. He vividly recalls pleading
beyond pleading for God to help Delores during her "attacks", but no help ever came. Alcohol, however, always
worked.

Over the years, alcohol began to fill in the missing parts
of his adopted self and to replace the wife he thought he
should have some relationship with. His new friend alcohol
filled the voids for years.

After these 13 years, Delores underwent a "spiritual experience" and claimed that she had spent the day with
Jesus. She quit cold-turkey all the medicine she had been
consuming daily, along with the alcohol she had drank in
enormous amounts. Then she demanded that David stop.

David had no intention of giving up the only friend he
had ever been able to depend on. The more she pressured
him, the more fearful he became of being forced to give up
his remedy. The effect was that his drinking increased, but
in secret.

Periodically, Delores caught him, either by smell or the
way he acted. Then he had to beg her forgiveness and

swear never to drink again. But he continued drinking alcoholically for more than five years after she had stopped.

Eventually David had to try to stop for his own sake. A friend of his who was a physician found that his liver was two-and-a-half times normal size; that his pancreas was malfunctioning; that certain reflexes were gone. The doctor said he would be dead in six months unless he quit immediately. But he could not stop. There was not enough left of David to rise to the task.

In the course of the marriage, the couple had four biological daughters. While pregnant with the fourth, Delores insisted on having a tubal ligation following the delivery. David hated the idea with a passion. He loved the children he had, and he believed that the procedure amounted to mutilation. Delores, backed by her therapist at the time, had the ligation anyway. By the time the youngest child was two or three, she began to complain bitterly that she could not have more children.

Soon after the youngest was 9, Delores wanted to adopt a baby with mixed racial background. David had no objection, and in fact welcomed the idea of another child. He realizes now that besides truly loving children, he had a hidden motive: that another child would keep his wife occupied.

She certainly needed something to occupy her. Ever since their first-born was 9 years old, Delores gave the children the responsibility of housekeeping, eventually including preparation of meals. She herself did nothing except for projects that amused her for a time. When she was in her early 20s, she worked for a month or so at a children's shelter, but quit when she became pregnant. Early in that pregnancy she was "suicidal" because she thought she was not pregnant.

Back to David's alcoholism. He managed to stay sober on one stretch for 10 straight years. But up until five and a half years ago, he had been detoxified, near death, four times. Each "slip," however, lasted only a few days before he turned himself in.

By adopting a second newborn daughter, again with mixed racial background, the couple became the parents of six daughters: four biological, and two adopted. The oldest four of the six are grown with children of their own. They remember their dad being drunk only a few times because he did not drink except during the brief relapses mentioned, and those did not last long.

What these daughters do not understand is that their father was not himself at any time during their formative years. They do not know that their father continued to live out the horrors of his life as a lost and incomplete person. They witnessed a personality, but not a person. It was not David, but his false self, his adopted self, that they grew up with.

David did not even begin a true discovery of his self until he gave up both alcohol and his wife for good. His final detoxification triggered what was to become a gradual realization of all the lies he had swallowed; all the manipulations he had endured; all the false guilt he had swallowed.

The last binge, as David now knows, was a veiled suicide attempt. He was hoping that he would never wake up, that he had consumed a lethal amount of alcohol. When he awoke in the detoxification facility, he paced the hall relentlessly until a nurse gave him a shot. He was in a state of nauseating depression, unbearable remorse, terror, and absolute helplessness. He wanted with everything in him to die, and as soon as possible.

He doesn't know whether anyone has ever wanted to die more than he did, but there was no way out, as usual. Not even death was an option, because he had let his life insurance lapse, and if he died, the family would have no income. He knew Delores would never work, and even if she did, she could never earn the income needed for their family. So here David was: a man with no life in him but forced to live.

The loudspeaker in the hall squawked that an A.A. (Alcoholics Anonymous) meeting was starting and that everybody had to attend. David sat down with the other men, dressed in pajamas and foam slippers, and then listened to the meeting begin. Then a strange thing happened. It occurred to him that maybe there was one more hope: that after all these years, this program of recovery might be able to teach him something that would finally work.

Later, while lying on his bed and staring at the paint peeling off the ceiling, while occasionally tracing a roach scurrying to find cover, he made a resolution. He committed himself to life, but it must be a very different life. David told himself that he had to change everything about his approach to living. He would put all of his beliefs, convictions, attitudes, desires—everything—up for scrutiny and a fresh look through the eyes of A.A. He would become open-minded about every new idea he would encounter. He did not realize it then, but his first and most important task was to find the real David.

Up until now, he had lived in terms of other people: what they believed; what they needed; what would make them happy. He understood other people very well, and he knew that he had been given some sort of a gift for helping people. But never had he given the slightest thought to finding himself.

When he was discharged and returned home, he acquired from seemingly no-where the freedom to disagree with some people he had never questioned before and conversely, to agree with some he had always been at odds with. Delores thought this was all a sign of instability—or maybe that's what she hoped. She had no idea that his eyes had been truly opened, and that he was not going back.

This new resolve, as stated, was the beginning of his getting well; that is, finding the truth about himself. He began to examine everything he had ever believed all over again, whether he had changed his mind on the subject already or not, and no matter how many times.

He found himself strongly disagreeing with Delores on various matters, especially child rearing, even though he had never dared before. He sensed that she had chosen a rut to remain in for the rest of her life and was not by any means going to join him in his life-enhancing adventure. Whether she came or not, he was on his way, for survival was the issue.

As time went on, David found he was angry at his wife most of the time, and vice-versa. He had begun to dread coming home from work, because even though she no longer hid in closets, she did not do much else either. But what bothered him the most was the way she treated their first adopted daughter, whom we'll name Amy. Delores, having become a fanatical, Pentecostal "Christian" years before, blamed demons for Amy's being a difficult child.

David realized that Amy had been a difficult child, but that Delores had always managed her in a wrong and sometimes crazy way, despite his protests. In fact, his objections only brought down the rage of his wife on both him and the child. So there had been no win.

One night, when the child was only four, David found her tied to a bookshelf by her pigtails, in which predicament the child was screaming and struggling desperately to get loose. Delores had said the child was full of demons and had the strength of ten men. David had promptly untied her and comforted the child, despite his wife's fury.

About five years ago, when Amy was only ten, Delores returned to drinking, but only before dinner. She would get extremely mellow, to put it mildly, and then after dinner, which made the buzz wear off, she became vicious toward both David and the children, but especially Amy. This activity was during David's first year after detoxification. She drank in front of him, and he admits buying her the alcohol. He says taking the chance of going into a liquor store was worth the risk in order to earn a brief period of peace during Delores' mellow period before dinner.

During a very rare heated encounter, David broke out with the words, "Shut the f— up!" Then he sprung on her the threat of divorce. Then he backed down and said he would work late and come home to see the children briefly before they went to bed; that he would sleep on the sofa, and see the children in the mornings before going to school. Delores insisted that he leave permanently. He did, that very night.

He says that leaving Delores was like leaving himself, for he hadn't known where he stopped and she began. He was unable to make himself go very far in distance, so he slept on the floor of his nearby office. His A.A. sponsor, as soon as he learned what had been happening, seized the opportunity to get David free before it was too late. For years the sponsor and other friends from A.A. had warned him that his sobriety was at stake unless he got away from her.

The sponsor took him to his own home, with his wife and child. It had taken the sponsor about three hours to convince David to come with him. He did not want to venture too far from the prison camp, just like the soldiers in World War II. Indeed, the overwhelming feeling that tortured David was that of being the worst traitor in the world. In the next few months, David lost 20 pounds due to feeling too guilty to eat.

It is a fact that alcoholism very often—and perhaps most often—follows abuse, whether mental, sexual, or physical. The alcoholic is the ultimate living example of a false self trying to survive without any real power. Alcoholics Anonymous can affect the discovery of one's true personhood.

A.A. helped David greatly as time went on. He found the obvious: that his own life was as important as anyone's—something he could never grasp before. He also, in time, underwent the revelation that he, and all of us, are supposed to be happy—that happiness, not misery, is the normal state of being. But the most important thing A.A. has done for David is to remove the fear of God as well as his preconceived ideas of who God is.

David relates:

> The first thing to understand about God is that you can't understand God. You must accept this. The second thing to get right is that you need Him. The third thing is that you are not

Him and you can't do his job. The fourth thing is that He is love. The fifth thing is that he is not a theologian.

Today, if someone were to ask me to define God, I would say that I wouldn't dare. I can't even define a human being. It would be much easier for me to say what He is not. He is not the God of wrath and punishment that I always, at heart, thought He was. I was afraid of Him all of my life. So I made another 'god,' out of alcohol.

In all my religious pursuits, I have never experienced Him, only heard about Him through the various opinions of some famous and some not so famous people who thought they knew Him. But when my very life was on the line, when I did not want to live anymore, I encountered His presence. He was in the midst of a room full of smoking, joking, non-pious, former drunks who loved each other and weren't ashamed to say it and prove it.

David had actually gone all the way back to adolescence and re-performed his developmental work regarding experimental identity and experimental power. His active participation in A.A., including the close friends he made, who were the first since adolescence, began to give him an identity. Comments at meetings helped greatly in obtaining new and accurate information about himself.

The spiritual component of A.A. enabled him to find a father replacement, which he termed "God, my Father." The new father justified his existence, and his belief initiated a search for purpose in his life. This time, he knew that his "calling" was not to keep Delores alive, nor to make her happy. The new meaning of his existence, as opposed to his previous misconception, had to be possible.

Just as male batterers do, female abusers continue to punish the former captive through whatever means they can find. Delores has maintained her manipulation through the courts as the divorce, even at this writing, continues.

About two years after the separation, David was returning from a meeting one night when he saw Delores and Amy sitting in a car waiting for him. They both approached, with Delores saying, "She's all yours. She's full of demons."

David was very happy about this surprise, because he loved his daughter very much, and he saw an opportunity to correct all the verbal, and sometimes physical, abuse Delores had put the child through. Amy was now about 12.

He was nowhere close to realizing that he had been presented with another impossible task. He was now in charge of an infuriated, defiant and vicious child, so full of hate that her rage spread to everyone, but especially to David, because now he was in charge. Just as lightning tends to strike the tallest object, rage always strikes the closest person. David had no idea that he was to go through hell because of what Amy would do. He was about to experience how some children, who have a very strong constitution, react to abuse: through outrageous behavior. They pay back.

Amy had been abandoned by her birth mother, her adoptive mother, and when David left, her adoptive father. Her rage exploded everywhere, and the rampage was to last for years.

First she began disrupting classes at school, then insulting teachers, then skipping school, then assisting in an apartment burglary, then running away for days at a time, then running away for weeks at a time, and finally running away for months at a time, taking haven in crack houses in the inner city. Her last long-term runaway was a full three months until she was picked up by police. She told the officers she had run away because her father had sexually abused her from the age of five.

Even though the officer from the sex crimes unit did not believe her, and in spite of the fact that the state attorney saw nothing in the case, the Florida Department of

Children and Families drew up a petition for dependency anyway. The petition violated the legalities regarding hearsay exception rules, but the court accepted the petition and granted it totally without evidence of any kind.

As an aside, it should be stated that child protective services agencies violate the law most of the time in presenting their petitions for dependency. There is no due process for the accused, and there is no way an innocent person can escape. Once the petition is granted, the child becomes a ward of the state. If the agency cannot build a criminal case against the accused, he is denied the right to have any kind of contact with any minor children.

In Jacksonville, Florida, Duval County's Juvenile Court goes along with a scam between the agency and certain favored psychologists in private practice who make their living from agency referrals. In order for the accused ever to be able to have contact with his children again, he must be "evaluated" by one of these few psychologists. If the accused maintains his innocence, he is labeled "in denial" and in need of two years of weekly therapy. If he admits to the alleged offense in order to complete the process and see his children again, he is labeled a "sex offender" in need of weekly therapy until the psychologist discharges him.

David chose not to play the game. Thus, he cannot have contact either with Amy (wherever she is) or with his younger adopted daughter, and certainly not his wife.

Delores seized upon this opportunity as being too good to be true, and immediately began a prolonged effort of convincing their grown children that David had done the same to them, but they just do not remember. She pressured and threatened the state attorney to arrest her husband. In fact, she harassed the man so often that he contacted David and said "Your wife is crazy." She also communicated the lie to the authorities governing David's profession, so that he was driven out of business. Then, when he fell behind in temporary alimony and child support, she tried to have him arrested for failure to pay.

What did the most damage to David was the fact that there is no way to disprove such an allegation. He believed that all of his children had a seed planted in their minds that he might actually be a pervert. Thus, he found it impossible to face any member of his family.

David deteriorated. Loss of his profession meant loss of a substantial part of his identity. Loss of his family was too much to bear. The threat of going to jail for unpaid child support was the final straw. He tried to kill himself.

He survived by a very narrow margin, and was then committed by the emergency department to a public psychiatric holding facility. From there, he managed to get himself to a distant state where his family of origin resides. With their very substantial help, he has been recovering for about seven months at this writing. The final divorce trial will probably occur in a few months.

In 2001, David became a priest of the Catholic Charismatic Church. He now serves hospitals and nursing homes as a volunteer chaplain plus continues his ministry of counseling.

11 Child Abuse Treatment

When I first moved to Jacksonville, Florida, from Philadelphia over 20 years ago, one of the first things I did was to purchase a boat. Unfortunately, I chose a second-hand model without knowing anything about how to fix it. Every time it broke down, and that seemed to be at least once a week, I needed to head straight to the parts department of the local marina store and buy another part that I hoped would make the engine run again. In time, I had spent more on parts than I had for the boat itself. When a friend found out what I had been doing, he said, "You can't do that. You have to find the problem and fix it."

The same principle needs to be applied in treating children who have been abused. Just as schools affix meaningless labels to children with learning or behavioral difficulties, many who attempt to treat children follow an inflexible model. A big part of the problem is that not enough is known about the impact of child abuse on the individual. Every "self" is different from every other. Even identical twins are far apart in the way they interpret and react to the very same life experiences.

Therefore, "child abuse" is no more a diagnosis than is "fever" for pneumonia or "anoxia" for a specific cognitive impairment. Every treatment plan must begin with an accurate diagnosis, not in the form of a label, but instead encompassing the major life factors the child has dealt with and will could face in the future, all in light of his present suffering.

The few adequate outcome studies on treatment reveal a miserable level of success, and it is my contention that the failure rate is due to the treatment methodologies being both over-standardized and based on too little information about what child abuse does to the individual child, in addition to general, categorized, diagnoses and lack of focus in treatment. After the review of 20 years' worth of studies, encompassing hundreds of thousands of sexually abused children, there is little evidence to support the belief that therapy facilitates recovery (Finkelhor and Berliner, 1995).

One of the largest obstacles to effective treatment, in my view, is that children do not fit well into medical-model diagnostic categories. By and large, children do not suffer from "mental illness" but instead react to the conditions of their lives. They form adjustments or maladjustments to reality. In order to help a child, it is necessary to pinpoint and do something about the life factors that are causing him to suffer, underperform, or misbehave.

If the diagnosis is both accurate and comprehensive, and the treatment is focused not on theory but on reality, then the child will respond, provided that the therapist knows how to treat abused children.

Most therapists, whether psychiatrists, psychologists, social workers, or mental-health counselors, have no idea how to treat abused children, because the subject is not taught in their graduate curriculum. The most prevailing mental-health issue of our time has not found its way to the graduate-school classroom. Any information so far developed has been gathered through individual research studies which must be "hunted down" by any professional interested in the subject.

Such organizations as the American Professional Society on the Abuse of Children (APSAC) and the International Society for Traumatic Stress Studies (ISTSS), to name my two favorites, should be joined by every professional in the field, including attorneys. Their journals should be standard reading.

Another factor sabotaging outcome results is that "therapy" has no end-point but instead continues on until the process becomes destructive rather than helpful. Prolonged, weekly encounters with the therapist can keep the original trauma alive, cause over-dependency on the therapist, and re-convince the child that there is something wrong with him, the very mindset that he came in with. The major goal is for the child to understand at the deepest level that the problem is outside of him. He is not the problem. The problem is that he has had to suffer needlessly, and a way must be found to improve his life circumstances. If these life circumstances are not changed, the child will continue to react.

In any therapy for any condition, it must always be remembered that there is no normal way to react to craziness in any form. Nor is there any normal way to react to maltreatment or neglect.

Therefore, the very first factor in forming a diagnosis and treatment plan is to find out what the child is reacting to, and this evaluation demands a thorough study of home life and the histories of the caregivers.

Next, the child must be set free from all blame. It cannot be emphasized strongly enough that the child believes that the maltreatment is his fault. Following that accomplishment, treating either trauma or information deficiencies will be necessary.

In the treatment of trauma, the damaging events must be brought to full consciousness, and then they must be recast in order to make sense for processing. Obviously, the establishment of a feeling of complete safety and trust is required, and for this reason, actual therapy may not begin immediately. Instead, the child should be allowed to play at something he truly enjoys, be it a video game, a board game with the therapist being a player, or whatever. Nothing can be accomplished until the child feels safe with the therapist.

This consideration brings up the matter of whether the therapist should be male or female, especially in cases where the child is female and the abuser is male. Ideally, since the harm was inflicted by a male, a more complete processing can be accomplished when the therapist is also male. Many times, however, this is not possible because the child is too upset. The factor must still be considered in the case of little boys, but with female children the importance is greater.

When the child has reached a level of comfort and safety, and he trusts the therapist, there is a technique that can be used to bring the traumatic events to the present with minimal upset. The child can be given a toy telescope to focus on a completely blank wall. As he is complying, suggestions of progressive relaxation can be given to bring the child to a relaxed state and heightened suggestibility. (Full-scale hypnosis is not recommended because in rare instances the child can become overwhelmingly upset when his defenses are down. Also, hypnotic recall does not hold up well in court.)

Next, it can be suggested that he is in his favorite place, where he feels safest of all, and where he is happy. He can be told that he is now looking at a movie of himself, but that he is still in the safe place. Now he can be asked about the bad parts of the movie. The child may go very far the first time, or he may not be able to comply at all, in which case the procedure is repeated later. He is informed that being able to play this "game" is a goal that will continue to be worked on. He should be praised for his hard work, no matter how much he has accomplished.

When the child has been able to describe the traumatic events, the time has arrived for a thorough discussion of them, with the emphasis on making sense for processing. Some meaning and explanation must be attached to these recollections so that the child can move past them. One form of talking about the trauma is the recommended interview for a forensic evaluation, as shown below. Known as the "cognitive interview", it is also very useful for court testimony when required (Walker, 1994).

> First, have the child reconstruct the circumstances of the crime by encouraging her to put herself in the place and time that the abuse occurred—e.g., "picture it as if you were there right now." To ensure the child focuses on actual events, do not use words "imagine," "pretend," or "story." Second, report everything the child says. Ask her to tell you as much information as pos-

sible, even seemingly unimportant details. After the child finishes her narrative description, follow with questions to clarify what was said. Third, go through the incident from beginning to end, then reverse the order and go through it again. Finally, encourage the child to recount events from different perspectives—e.g., "if you were sitting in the corner of the room, what would you have seen?"

Again, the above procedure is to be performed only after the child has mastered the telescope task. This process of the child's recounting the abuse from different perspectives and repeating the account more than once, not only opens possibilities for explanatory discussion but also tends to desensitize the child's internal responses.

Next, the child can be assisted in writing a letter to the abuser, without holding back any words of emotional expression. The child is assured that whether the letter is mailed or not will be decided later, and the decision will be his alone.

When neglect rather than direct abuse is at issue, the therapist should engage the child in play and praise the child for everything done—or at least comment on every activity. Ongoing interaction with positive regard is the thrust. A goal is for the child to be convinced that an important adult truly cares about him and is interested in what he says and does.

Beyond this goal, it is necessary to work with educators and social workers to ensure placement in a stimulating milieu where praise, appropriate affection, and plentiful attention will be guaranteed. In most cases, if the child is placed in a foster home, it will be better if the child is the only one in care, at least for several months.

If the "Inventory for Concealed Child Abuse" (page 37) has been used prior to therapy, it can again be given for comparison. A significant reduction in the number of positive responses could help form a possible measure of outcome.

One further thought here is that almost any form of child treatment demands a team approach. Social-service agencies, educators, school counselors, pediatricians, and perhaps child-advocacy attorneys are some of the resources that must be relied on heavily. In this regard, it is absolutely essential that these people have a firm understanding of what the child's needs are, what the therapist is trying to accomplish, and why. Also, it should be cautioned that if court testimony is required, the therapist must speak in plain English, in an open and relaxed manner, with "psycho-babble" avoided at all costs.

12 Domestic Abuse Treatment

Most of my domestic-abuse survivors have a history of multiple abusive ("romantic") relationships beginning in adolescence and continuing into adulthood. When there is an exception, the survivor has found a man of endless patience who is willing to endure the extremely trying behavior that resembles a borderline personality disorder. This is the case because most are suffering from post-traumatic stress disorder (PTSD) or a symptomatic picture closely resembling it.

Judith Herman (1992) boldly exposes the rampant misdiagnoses of trauma victims and calls the overlooked diagnosis of posttraumatic stress disorder an epidemic. To be discussed shortly, the diagnosis of borderline personality disorder is one of the most insulting that any doctor could pick from the list of diagnostic criteria.

My male survivors tend to fall into one of several descriptive categories: hostility toward women in general due to abuse by their mothers; past criminal activity, always associated with alcohol or drugs; PTSD; or any combination of the above. With few exceptions, the men are of above-average to high intelligence, but working in low-level jobs and are completely blinded as to their true selves and potential. Occasionally, a man will present with a previous history of either schizophrenia or bi-polar psychotic illness, and their symptoms, if considered in isolation, somewhat justify such a misdiagnosis.

Regardless of gender, prior misdiagnoses are most often found in the patients with the most severe childhood trauma, combined with the least recall of what happened.

According to Dr. Herman, who received the Guttmacher Award by the American Psychiatric Association, abuse victims are falling through the cracks when it comes to correct diagnosis and treatment. She propounds that up to

60 percent of psychiatric patients, both in-patient and out-patient, report childhood histories of physical or sexual abuse or both. This estimate excludes emotional abuse and neglect. She believes, and my experience confirms, that these patients are suffering from PTSD as a direct result of childhood maltreatment.

Some psychologists and psychiatrists know what to expect in the way of symptomatology with war veterans: PTSD. We know as a fact that, even in the strongest individual, the experiences of war can produce the constellation of symptoms that therapists should recognize as trauma. But for some reason, we have only begun to make this same connection with people whose lives have been a "war".

One woman, Catherine, spent nearly 20 years in therapy, first with an educational counselor, then three psychiatrists, plus a family therapist, found herself with suicidal feelings right up to the time she entered our group for domestic abuse. One psychiatrist, an analyst, spent two years asking her, "What do you think?" Another psychiatrist gave her open prescriptions for highly addictive drugs, and the third psychiatrist wanted to use electro-convulsive therapy, probably the worst possible treatment for trauma survivors. The family therapist ordered her to draw a family genealogy chart.

None of the above professionals seemed determined to find the cause of her suffering; they just had their favorite ways of treating symptoms. Catherine's real problem had been nightly incest at the hands of her biological father, the rejection by her mother as a result, and constant debasing comments by both parents and both sisters all of her life. Not even her head-banging, a dead giveaway for sexual abuse, was noticed.

Another woman, Lynn, was in treatment for 30 years for depression and "borderline personality disorder," 10 of these years with the same psychiatrist. When the decade had passed, he remarked, "I really don't think I can help you." Never was Lynne's sadistically violent tormentor, her husband, ever asked about or seen.

None of her therapists had been interested in causality. A disinterest in root cause is, in my opinion, the greatest weakness in the mental-health professions. We have clung so closely to the medical model that emotional disturbances of most any kind have historically been seen as free-standing, as though they had arisen from an infection, from a vacuum, or from nowhere. How this mentality has survived is a mystery, when in any other science the principle of cause and effect rules.

Put another way, for every action there is a reaction. Molest, torture, humiliate, or neglect a child severely enough, and PTSD or similar symptoms will be the reaction. For this reason, the treatment of domestic abuse is the treatment of child abuse, and both are the treatment of trauma. Here are some of the diagnostic indicators of PTSD (American Psychiatric Association, 1994):

- The patient has experienced a life-threatening or unspeakable event involving self or someone close or has lived through a horrible period in life.
- The response consisted of fear, helplessness, or horror.
- The event(s) is re-experienced even though it may have occurred long ago; for example:
  - Memories, images, flashbacks.
  - Nightmares.
  - Feeling as though the event is happening now.
  - Numbing or freezing of emotions.
  - Dissociation.
  - Intense distress triggered by reminders.
- Avoidance behavior is exhibited; for example:
  - Avoiding thoughts, feelings, conversations regarding the event(s).
  - Avoiding people, places, things that trigger emotion.
- Inability to recall an important part of the event.
- Diminished interest in normal activities.
- Feeling detached from others.

- Restricted range of emotions or episodic rage.
- Sense of foreshortened future.
- Hyperarousal, including:
    o Difficulty falling or staying asleep.
    o Irritability.
    o Difficulty concentrating.
    o Hypervigilance.
    o Exaggerated startle response.
- Depersonalization.
- Derealization.

Notice the reference to an "inability to recall an important part of the event." Despite all the controversy, repressed memories are an actuality found frequently in abuse survivors. This phenomenon, I believe, can be explained cognitively if one considers two things: 1) a child cannot process an event that makes no sense or that is too overwhelming for his interpretation; and 2) dissociation, a natural defense common to all children, blocks out most of the memory so that any recall will be weak at best.

There is a way to determine whether a memory is valid or not. If the recall of a terrifying or unspeakable event is valid, the result will usually be relief rather than further terror, provided that the recall occurs in a supportive environment. Conversely, "false memories," or those instigated by the therapist, will usually upset the patient even more. This is not to say that accurate recall will, of itself, be curative, but it will bring great comfort and encouragement even though cognitive processing, desensitization, and other measures must follow successfully. Recall brings relief because it brings with it an explanation.

Without exception, every patient I have ever treated for anything, all through my 20 years of practice, has had a basis in reality for the symptoms, as serious as they may have been.

Sometimes part of the reality lies in genetic predisposition, such as with alcoholism, schizophrenia, and bi-polar illness. Often there are strong biochemical factors that must be dealt with pharmacologically. But these biologic factors, as important as they are, do not explain every-thing.

Why, for example, have the schizophrenics I've treated been raised either in chaos or in an environment where there has been no communication? How does one learn to think when no-one has taught him? What else can the child use as a navigation system besides his feelings, with his emotions being his only guide in how to react? Also, if put under enough stress, everyone will break. The nature of the resulting pattern depends on genetic weaknesses, which all of us have, but they vary among people. So, if the family situation is bad, one person may end up schizophrenic, another depressed, etc.

As a further example, and the most important for the purposes of this book, let us look at the criteria for border-line personality disorder (American Psychiatric Association, 1994) in light of child abuse and resultant trauma. (APA criteria are indented, and my comments appear in plain text.)

Borderline Personality Disorder

A pervasive pattern of instability of interpersonal relationships, self-image, and affects, and marked impulsivity beginning by early adulthood and present in a variety of contexts, as indicated by five (or more) of the following:

Frantic efforts to avoid real or imagined abandonment. Note: Do not include suicidal or self-mutilating behavior covered in criterion 5.

An abused child has been denied the full exploration of the true self, as well as imaginary becoming and the taste of power. A neglected child has been abandoned repeatedly in real life.

A pattern of unstable and intense interpersonal relationships characterized by alternating between extremes of idealization and devaluation.

The abused child's first relationships were the cause of shame, debasement, pain, and terror. The trust-versus-mistrust developmental process has been sabotaged. Abused children typically end up in a series of abusive relationships in late adolescence and both early and late adulthood.

Identity disturbance: markedly and persistently unstable self-image or sense of self.

Child abuse and neglect eradicate personhood and cause the formation of a false self that operates either on the illusion of power of the illusion of powerlessness. The true self is covered up beyond recognition.

Impulsivity in at least two areas that are potentially self-damaging (e.g., spending, sex, substance abuse, reckless driving, binge eating). Note: Do not include suicidal or self-mutilating behavior covered in Criterion 5.

Besides the problem-solving goal in sexually acting out, sex is a cheap substitute, or "quick fix" for the love a deluded person thinks is impossible to acquire. Substance abuse occurs in the majority of cases involving incest. Both binge eating and spending are, as patients themselves report, an effort to fill the emptiness they feel inside.

Recurrent suicidal behavior, gestures, or threats, or self-mutilating behavior.

Patients traumatized by severe child abuse report sudden suicidal urges and compulsions to harm themselves (especially symbolic, surface cutting of the wrist area) when they are overcome with the original message of being bad. The suppressed rage that naturally occurs as a result of the atrocities they have suffered will, at times when it breaks through the mental restraints, be aimed at self as a type of "substitute murder" whereby one's own self is killed rather than the abuser.

Affective instability due to a marked reactivity of mood (e.g., intense episodic dysphoria, irritability, or anxiety usually lasting a few hours and only rarely more than a few days).

These are "flashback" reactions triggered by reminders of the original abuse. The surge of feelings resembles one's listening to an old song on the radio whereby the exact emotional tone of the time returns completely. The mood reaction dissipates when the flashback is no longer fresh in the mind.

Chronic feelings of emptiness.

My traumatized patients report always feeling empty, with the emptiness most acute at times when they feel completely out of touch with any sense of being. Depersonalization, a consequence of abuse, leads to derealization, including the feeling of being empty inside- as though "no one is home."

Inappropriate, intense anger or difficulty controlling anger (e.g., frequent displays of temper, constant anger, recurrent physical fights).

Not only anger, but also rage, are primary symptoms of trauma. While male survivors tend to be direct and aggressive at times, women are more typically passive, with their anger being expressed through manipulation or complaining, sometimes alternating with depression.

Transient, stress-related paranoid ideation or severe dissociative symptoms.

Hypervigilance, severe enough to appear paranoid, is a primary symptom of trauma. And no wonder, since these victims have been betrayed, hurt, insulted, debased, and mangled without warning their entire lives. Dissociation occurs often during the time of the original abuse due to the fact that the child does not have the mental resources to comprehend the horrors that are being inflicted. The child finds that "going away" mentally is an effective way to deal with terror, and the practice continues into adulthood.

Thus it can be seen that this so-called personality disorder can be, at least in many cases, a reaction to the utterly absurd or unbearable. Seeing not just the above criteria but those of other personality disorders in this light raises a very provocative question: Are many forms of mental illness a reaction? Not putting aside biological and chemical factors, does this "reaction" concept fill in some voids in beginning to understand this unwieldy, mysterious, ill-defined matter we call "mental illness?"

If a child is raised in an abusive or neglectful environment, could anyone put together a reasonable description of what a normal response would be? Is there a normal way to respond to the preposterous or to outright craziness? Is there a "correct" way to adapt to what M. Scott Peck terms "evil?"

Trauma symptoms, as Herman courageously puts forth, are the end result of child abuse. Place a strong and brave soldier in combat that is terrifying enough, horrifying enough, painful enough, intense enough, and long enough, and a "classic" trauma picture will emerge. Is this hero mentally ill?

One beginning principle that helps give patients hope in their early treatment of domestic abuse is the indestructibility of the "self". My treatment regimen strongly encourages spirituality, but certainly not religion, which I see as potentially destructive. Belief in the supernatural, however, facilitates the overcoming of powerlessness and rejection. I go so far as to liken the self with the Judeo-Christian concept of the "soul" and its eternal nature. Seen from this point of view, the self can be mangled but not destroyed.

The soul can be fooled, betrayed, injured, abandoned, and tortured beyond endurance, but it cannot be killed. No matter how thoroughly bashed a soul has been, it can be revived when the lies of abuse are systematically removed... when the false messages are dissected one by one and replaced with valid discoveries about one's true self.

Group Therapy

When the early communications that still live in the brain are put on trial, and the credentials of those "experts" who implanted the ideas are challenged by a group, the roots of delusion are loosened and eventually pulled. Then there remains fertile soil in which to plant the truth: the indisputable facts of one's own successes and talents never before considered are explored and brought to life.

Similarly, the process of discovering one's true self is facilitated by the examination of one's values. I can think of no other factor that more describes the true self than one's value system. Typically, as one powerful exercise, I take out a sheet of paper and write down the traits that the patient admires in other people, be they celebrities or people they have come to learn about or know well during their lives. When the list is complete, I hand it back to the patient and instruct her to write her own name at the top. Then I ask her to affix it to her refrigerator or bedroom mirror and add to it daily, every time she thinks of something else,

Many a patient has held another person in awe due to some very positive characteristics of a personal or characterological, nature. Those qualities admired in another person are already one's own. Such is self-evident. How could another's attributes be valued unless the value itself is part of one's own true nature? All patients see the point very clearly.

Patients are uniformly buoyed by the realization that there is an understandable explanation for why they are in their present state of suffering—that their condition does not have to remain shrouded in mystery, and especially that they are not hopelessly mentally ill or otherwise inferior to other people. I tell every patient I see that we'll together come to know the cause of the distress and then go to work to "fix" it. The adage, "Knowing the problem is half the solution" is gloriously true in psychotherapy, no matter what the presenting condition.

Effective treatment cannot proceed until the patient is first comfortable with the therapist and then comfortable in the therapy group. In the group, which I have found to be the most effective method, as have many others, there must be certain ground rules. Importantly, no-one is ever encouraged to speak about herself until she really wants to share. No group member may criticize or insult another. All members must give a genuinely warm welcome to new-comers (and they do, from the heart). Each member must commit to attendance each time (once a week for 90 minutes, with a break after 45 minutes).

Also, the group must be small, preferably not more than 10. After that number, a new group is begun. It is vital that the group be stabilized so that all members know each other well and have no fear of another member. They are encouraged to exchange phone numbers and use them often in order to establish an enduring emotional resource.

Typically, the group becomes so cohesive that they plan social events together in addition to going out to eat after the sessions. They visit each other when sick, and call an absent member to make sure she is all right. All of this is done out of genuine concern for each other. In other words, they become closer than sisters.

A newcomer will usually remain silent for a session or two before she begins to share. But when the time comes, she experiences an immediate partial healing because for the first time in her life she is able to have her feelings and her prior behavior understood and validated. All of her life, she has been told to minimize her trauma and "just get over it." However, this has always been impossible because the events of her life have made no sense and therefore could not be processed. Besides that, similar events keep happening, over and over.

When she finds a group of women who have suffered in very similar ways, and they say, "I understand, and I feel what you feel," her life-long search to connect with another person has finally succeeded. She feels as though she has been touched and made into a person entitled to her feelings, reactions and behaviors.

Usually, a patient will address one or members of the group when she is talking, rather than the therapist. The therapist, however, directs the course of the discussion and frequently intercedes with insights or explanations. He acts as a protector for all members and jumps in at the slightest hint of anything threatening to anyone. When the conversation becomes too intense, he switches to a lighter subject and then later returns to the difficult matter.

When the group is first initiated, the therapist spends several sessions explaining what trauma is and how it is the natural result of abuse. He further shows that child abuse typically leads to abusive relationships in later life. The therapist is accompanied by a female co-facilitator, in our case an experienced psychiatric nurse who is very motherly.

As the group addresses actual experiences of the members, the sessions are alternated so that after a session of intense sharing, the next session is devoted to a lighter subject.

Each session brings reports of new power acquisition in their interpersonal affairs; that is, examples of self-assertion or simply doing something kind for one's self. Since abuse results in powerlessness, the acquisition of power on many fronts helps propel the course of therapy and provides the courage to examine the past.

There must come a time of life when a person turns around and takes a look back to ask the question, "Were my parents correct about me? Did they give me the truth about who I really am, or did they give me messages distorted by who they were?" We must be adventurous, full of courage, in order to decide what information to keep and what to throw out. We must find out who we are in fact.

Those who are spiritually minded begin by finding out *why* they are, and this discovery tends to lead to *who* they are. Many come to believe that a life plan has been prearranged for them by their supreme being, and that they have a special place in this world. All are therefore encouraged constantly to explore any hidden talents or abilities that they may have thought about as small children sitting on the back steps just daydreaming. Back then, what was possible did not matter. I want them to go back there and reconnect with their early, positive daydreaming of what they imagined could be.

As a result, I have repeatedly seen talents blossom. One lady is pursuing ballet; another is representing herself in court in a lawsuit against her abuser; a third is drawing brilliant political cartoons for several newspapers. They all have untouched, unrealized talents that are now undergoing exploration. These abilities, of course, add more information about the real self.

The participants are encouraged to comfort one another, not by advice-giving but by acceptance, and very often a barrage of hugs.

Recently a dear lady in our group was struggling in great pain over having been raped five times, all by different men she had grown to trust. She was helped to understand that it was her *first* rape, at 15, that caused the second, that caused the third, and so on. Rapists are predators, and predators, by their very nature, go after wounded prey. Vultures can spot disabled targets from a very great distance in the sky.

The same is true of all abusers. They prey on the wounded. One man now in treatment just had to know—was driven to know—why his adoptive father hated him but not his siblings. The answer is quite direct: His siblings had never been wounded, but this boy had been. He had spent his first two years of life in neglectful foster care before being adopted. By the time of his adoption, the main vulture in his life had him well marked for the kill.

Those members of the group who have proven that they feel safe enough to interact are often asked about any present distress. Then the current hurt is traced to an original message communicated in some way in childhood. We ask the question, "What is this pain wired to?" They are taught to visualize actual wires connecting their present discomfort to a real event earlier and, importantly, to the *person* at the end of the wire.

They learn to identify whose voice they hear when they believe they are themselves inflicting the pain. They name the voice when they are compelled to put themselves down or harm themselves, and they come to appreciate the "magical power" of the phantom "renting space" in their heads. They are helped to defy the commands of the abuser's voice and are rewarded with lavish applause and affection every time they disobey. When they feel terror or helplessness, we ask which lie they are honoring.

On and on, they continue their search for the inner child, the real self, before the sacred product underwent tampering. They are not looking for a new person, but an old one who remains young: the person they already are but have yet to realize and celebrate.

As previously explained, when prisoners of war are released, the do nut run for freedom but stay huddled at the center of the camp. Freeing the prisoners is not sufficient. Having them grasp the reality of their freedom, that they are already free, is what restores their liberty.

So it is with domestic abuse survivors. They remain prisoners of lies because the truth has not reached their hearts. They crouch in fear, loathing not themselves but who they think they are. They are unaware that the real self is alive and available for wondrous exploration.

They are just waking from slumber and wiping their eyes as they only peek at the light one small glimpse at a time. Now they merely sense an opening, but one day they will walk out the door.

13 Special Populations

Discussed in this chapter are two of the groups most vulnerable to child abuse: inner-city children living in gross impoverishment, both economically and culturally; and those children with attention-deficit, hyperactivity disorder (ADHD).

Cultural Deprivation

Of all the minority groups in the United States, black children trapped in a "ghetto" mentality are the most subject to every kind of child abuse. Their high-risk status arises from cultural deprivation as a result of the present generation still living the effects of slavery that supposedly ended with the Civil War. Although the war made slavery illegal, it did not remove the generational effects.

Slavery utterly destroyed the black family. Men and women were kept in separate barracks, and not even partnerships were permitted, let alone marriages. Men and women were forced to "mate" like animals. Plantation owners were breeders of beings they did not consider human. The masters "reared" the offspring only in the sense of teaching obedience to the master.

Because slavery continued for generations, the captives, when set free after the war, had no concept of a black family. They had never seen one nor heard of one. They did not even know that they could form such a thing as a family.

Bigotry continues long after the abolishment of slavery, and right up to the present day. Only in very recent years has this population had an opportunity for education. Even now it is only theoretically possible for every black citizen to receive an education.

The fact that the "fences are down" has not fully penetrated the pockets of deep, long-lasting poverty within the
inner city of every major metropolitan area.

One might assume that small children encountered in
these neighborhoods would be found to be hostile. However, the fact is that the predominant mood is shame.
Among older people, the norm is serious religious conviction, a kind and compassionate "mellowness", and an
absence of bitterness over having lived a restricted life. If
we look at the very young and the old, we find blacks, even
in these conditions, to be gentle people.

I have formed these observations through years of
working with AIDS victims in a program I began in order to
serve them at home. Day after day, I entered such sections
of Jacksonville, Florida, and encountered people of all
ages. Even the teenagers became friendly, when they knew
I was there to help. This is not to say that I was not frightened at first, because I was. White people are afraid of
black people, and they have good reason to be.

Somewhere deep down in every decent white, there is a
realization, though it may be covered up, that our ances-
tors caused these conditions in the first place and allowed
them to prevail. Further, it is a fact that more crimes, except for white-collar, are committed by blacks, as the daily
newspapers and TV keep reminding us. The time is generations overdue for the white man to ask *why*; then to
ask *what can be done?*

Even though this is not a good time to begin change,
with the white families of every color on the endangered
list, we must begin. Ours must be the generation that
helps. Part of the "why" has already been described.
Blacks have lacked a family structure. Even though today
single-parent families are very prevalent in the white population, as are "partnerships," these phenomena have
produced dire consequences for blacks. The absence of a
father is child neglect at its worst.

The greater the poverty, the greater the shame of the
small children in the black population. What else could we
expect to see? We know already that neglect or other

abuse results in the child's taking the blame on himself. Black children begin their lives believing that they already have all that they deserve. Their predicament is *cultural abuse.*

When they enter school, they must face head-on the reality that they are not wanted there, that at least some people don't like them, are afraid of them, or even hate them. The greatest struggle of all begins when the experimental becoming of adolescence arrives.

Without a father, the black male teen has no "welcome to manhood." Yet he is male, and he knows that whatever his identity, it must conform to what his idea of male is. By prior example, therefore, he begins this stage of development with guidelines that have never worked. He sees adult males in any deprived culture impregnate women as though they are doing them a favor and then disappear. He sees grandmothers raising children, while the mothers go out and work at very low-level jobs. He sees his white schoolmates enjoying a much higher standard of living, and comes to the solid realization that he has been cheated.

Adolescent development largely takes the form of protest and defiance. Why should he honor the rules of such a society? The process of development propels him to find further identity plus an experimental personality that will work in the peer group. But the peers he must join and be accepted by are also defiant, and many are enraged. His clique fights with others and commits crimes.

Contrary to white teens, the black youngster has a very constricted choice of cliques. There is little likelihood that he will find a solidly-established group of black teen scholars, although thankfully he may find a group of athletes. But even if he identifies with the athletes, and is accepted, what about his mind? Where is the opportunity for him to be nourished intellectually so that he may become a desperately needed leader one day?

The process is quite similar with adolescent girls in the inner-city culture. Many have the idea that being impregnated by a boy is a compliment, even an honor, although he remains in her life only for a short time. Her education is interrupted in order to work at a fast-food restaurant while her mother raises the child. Not only that, but her own mother may have been through many rotating boy-friends, a certain percentage of whom have been abusive. Taking abuse from a male and being abandoned is a normal part of being a woman. Having a child is all a girl needs.

Many thousands of men and women have overcome these obstacles and achieved a fulfilling life. They have done their part to stop the cycle. But thousands of exceptions are still not enough, because only a very few are communicators who attempt to bring change within their own community. Not since Dr. Martin Luther King has there been a spokesman with as much charisma and *courage* to make a significant difference in the hope level of the deprived portion of the black culture.

Hope is needed more than anything. Next to that is education targeted specifically at changing the mindset of the ghetto. It is very significant that values and character are starting to be taught in public schools. But not until the present generation of parents and grandparents understands the "why", and what can be done, will there be visible improvement in this plight.

Black ministers, elected officials, physicians, educators and other professionals must become vocal and speak specifically to the problem: the absence of family and, more exactly, the mindset of teens.

Whites should attempt to overcome their fear and mistrust of blacks by facing the real danger: what will happen to us all if the black family remains unformed and the white family follows the same path. Our society has a greater danger than crime: We face extinction unless the family is reformed on solid ground.

Every white person in power, including members of the news media, should be in search of black spokespersons and should offer every possible opportunity for them to convey these messages. Black supervisors in industry should be afforded plentiful opportunities to speak to their workforce.

Popular music groups and movie stars should be outspoken about the issues, not by endless complaining about injustice, as real as it is, but by addressing in the most forceful way the solutions.

The white community must change its attitude. Some researchers have tried to prove a difference in intelligence levels between the two races but have ended up with well-deserved egg on their faces. The greatest resource in the entire world is all but untapped: the enormous population of black people and the inestimable contribution they have already made and can make further to the benefit of us all.

Anyone examining science, the professions, music, drama, writing, business, and the arts in general—or any other field—must admit that we have a priceless resource in the black community that has already emerged but can, in the future, blossom even more in every institution and setting throughout the world.

Attention–Deficit Hyperactivity Disorder

Well over 20 years ago, I noticed an obscure little article in an esoteric journal that discussed this subject, ADHD. I cannot find a reference to it, although I have searched everywhere, and none of my colleagues have ever heard of it either. If the author will come forward, due reference and credit will be given. What I do know is that the premise of that piece is very, very true.

In taking that small amount of information and adding my experience with children over all these years, I have come to believe that this condition is physiological and *not* psychological. It has become a "garbage-can" diagnosis overly used when an evaluator has not looked for causality, so that many children with this label do not have this condition at all but are instead suffering from PTSD as the result of child abuse.

Actual ADHD, according to my experience, is caused by sensory deprivation or restriction of movement during the period from infancy to about age 3. I have yet to find a case of this condition where a child has not either undergone some necessary medical procedure or suffered abuse resulting in one or more of the major senses being blocked for a prolonged period of immobilization. Many an accident has also caused such blocking.

Interfering with the perceptive senses or movement produces an "overcharged" central nervous system, whereby energy continues to build until there is an outlet. When this physiological change occurs, it remains permanent throughout the lifespan. The result is that movement and perceptual stimulation are required in excess. If these are not supplied at frequent intervals, the child becomes irritable, then angry, and finally enraged.

Besides hyperactivity, the constellation of symptoms includes being stubborn, having a "short fuse" when it comes to temper, defiance, and a strong liking for very loud music or other noise, as well as every form of physical stimulation, including touch. This may include very hot or very cold showers and back rubs; and activities that stimulate any of the senses, such as video games, sports, and almost any kind of exercise.

Some of the leading causes are surgery during infancy that requires strapping the baby down; orthopedic corrective devices, such as bars; prolonged confinement to an incubator; and even a difficult delivery whereby the baby is trapped in the birth canal. Tubes in the ears to correct hearing infections, procedures done to the eyes, and immobilization of any part of the body or the entire body are also included.

Why these procedures have this effect is not known. It is my understanding that when ulcer medications were being researched, it became necessary to produce ulcers in laboratory animals in order to test the trial medication. Researchers found that if they tied together the hind legs of any laboratory animal soon after birth, then an ulcer would develop within two or three days. Importantly, it was noted that the animal behaved in a hyperactive manner and further, that in later months it was not able to learn the tasks that the other animals learned, such as pushing a lever for a food pellet. Still more importantly, the animals thus restrained as newborns remained with these handicaps for the remainder of their lives.

Obviously, the animals did not have a psychological or emotional problem; they were not mentally ill. They had undergone a physiological change that altered their central nervous system.

With children, stimulation at very frequent intervals is an absolute necessity. For example, a young man in his junior year of high school had a life-long ambition of attending a certain university. Because of this condition, however, he was in trouble most of the time, and he could not concentrate in class. He was failing. No matter how hard he tried, he was not able to stay focused in the classroom nor even to sit still.

He had been born prematurely and thus had been confined to an incubator for weeks. Not only that, but he was immobilized inside the device so that feeding tubes and the like would remain in place. All of his life, he had been hyperactive and easily angered, but once he "exploded," he would settle down quickly. He loved burning-hot showers and loud music. By early adolescence he had gotten very down on himself because he seemed to be irritable most of the time. He was ashamed of himself and felt tremendous guilt over snapping at his parents and siblings.

When it was revealed to him that his problem was physical and not mental—further, that he was not responsible—there were tears of relief. I instructed him to get a portable radio with headphones and to play it every time he started to become irritable; also to take plenty of hot showers and to ask his mother to rub his back.

But the most important thing I did for this young man was to talk to an open-minded and cooperative counselor at his high school. She issued him a special pass that allowed him to go outside and run around the entire school building between classes.

The results were optimum. In fact, he did graduate with a grade average sufficient for admission to the university of his choice. Once he was in college, he had much more freedom and knew well what to do for himself; that is, how to manage his condition.

Many times I have asked an unbelieving mother in my office to take her son (or daughter), who was running around the room, and begin to scratch his back. Time after time, the child would settle down. Then I would have the child do some jumping jacks until he felt tired. When the stimulation and exercise had been completed, the child behaved normally. I must repeat, however, that such measures are required on an hourly basis or more, depending on severity.

Some experimentation is required to find the most effective form of stimulation. One 10-year-old boy, when he became wildly out of control, could be calmed only by hot showers.

One might ask why this topic is included in this book. One reason is that hyperactive children receive more abuse than those without this problem. More importantly, however, it must be pointed out that neglect can easily produce this life-long condition. A child not fed when hungry is deprived of the sense of taste, and the strong sense of hunger goes unsatisfied. Similarly, a child confined to a crib is denied full movement, as is a child forced to remain in a stroller or high chair long beyond his endurance. Some children are locked in closets or tied down as punishment. In short, a parent who purposely does not meet a child's needs as they occur is committing neglect. All needs are naturally occurring, and neither a child nor an adult can control when a need will arise. Because children cannot meet their own needs, a parent must. All kinds of consequences can follow when needs are not met.

14 The Dangerous Student

It has been stated that in my experience, children who are abused do not grow up to be abusers themselves. However, it is clear that youngsters entering school, as well as those already enrolled, can be explosive. Such is the case because certain individuals, depending on the type of abuse plus their own constitutions can be made mentally ill in a way that can present an imminent danger to the young person himself or two other students, as well as to teachers. Columbine and similar tragedies have taught us this lesson. For these reasons, I have included screenings that can bring attention to students who are suffering and who could possibly be dangerous.

The questionnaires presented beginning on p. 150 and p. 155 are experimental and preliminary. Several prominent institutions are testing these instruments at this writing for reliability and validity. Others are invited. The content validity is derived from 20 years of personal experience by the author and his colleagues, plus generally accepted factors spread throughout the literature.

Student Critical Symptoms Questionnaire

For grades 3 through 12 and 1st year college.

Instructions for Administration

All questions are to be read aloud by the examiner and answered "yes" or "no" by the student. Positive responses indicate a risk to some degree because every question can prompt an abnormal "yes" response.

This is a PRELIMINARY effort to develop a valid test, but in its present stage of development, it can *give only clues*. The number of positive responses justifying further evaluation by a qualified psychologist has yet to be established. However, the examiner may give added weight to certain responses, according to the examiner's own best judgment, especially if experienced and if familiar with examinee's history. Questions can be repeated upon request.

Before administration, put the student at ease by explaining that this is a routine test to determine anything special that the school can do to make him/her comfortable. State that this questionnaire may not be necessary in his/her case, but that all students are given this opportunity, especially when new to the school, and that it is for their benefit.

Say to student, "Here are some questions I'm going to ask. Some may sound strange, but don't let that bother you. Remember that this questionnaire is given to many people, and everybody's background is different. Please answer "yes" or "no", whichever comes to you first. Try not to hesitate. Let's begin. This won't take long."

Questions

1. I have been beaten up.
2. I don't know if I want to be ignored or not.
3. I daydream about getting even.
4. Very few people can understand me.
5. I've been insulted again and again.
6. If people knew my real powers, they'd respect me.
7. Most students are mean.
8. I dreamed I paid back the people who hurt me.
9. I have no reason to respect my teachers.
10. Some people don't deserve to live.
11. My mind has very special powers.
12. There are weapons in my home—at least one.
13. I've thought of using a weapon on my enemies.
14. I don't want to be like other people.
15. If people knew how important I am, they would admire me.
16. I'd feel better if some people left me alone.
17. There's no use talking to my mother or father.
18. I have a brother or sister who gets better treatment than I do.
19. It would suit me fine if I never had to go home.
20. Coming to school is very hard for me.
21. I hate for the other kids to see me naked in the locker room.
22. I think that all people are animals deep down.
23. When I'm home, I rarely come out of my room.
24. There are secrets about me that nobody will ever know.
25. My favorite video or internet games are very violent.
26. I love movies where there's plenty of bloodshed.
27. I'm not loved at home the way most kids are.

28. The way other students act is stupid.

29. There are people who "have it in" for me.

30. Some people are planning bad things for me.

31. I know that one day, I'll get justice.

32. I have powers that people don't know about.

33. I am extremely brilliant, but others can't recognize it.

34. Words can hurt almost as much as physical pain.

35. I try hard to avoid certain people.

36. I freeze in place and don't move for a while.

37. I lose the look on my face so nobody can tell what I'm feeling.

38. I have rolled up in a ball on the floor a lot, or in bed.

39. I have banged my head against the wall or the back of my bed.

40. Some people can read your mind.

41. It's possible to be controlled by somebody else or something else.

42. I daydream or stare off into space a lot.

43. I forget what I'm doing.

44. I don't feel pain when something should hurt.

45. I feel afraid but don't know why.

46. Sometimes I have greater power than anybody.

47. I often feel guilty without knowing why.

48. I worry about my temper.

49. Breaking things in a rage is not unusual for me.

50. I try very hard to be perfect.

51. Some people are perfect.

52. I have gotten so mad at people that I have worried about myself.

53. In school, I don't want to be part of any group.

54. The groups in this school are stupid.

55. I almost never feel guilty.

56. I can feel afraid, mad, and sad all at once.

57. I've felt like hurting myself on purpose.

58. Some people think I'm a nothing.

59. Some people think I'm weird.

60. I've done dangerous things, where I knew I would get hurt.

61. I believe strongly in the right to own a gun.

62. There are some secrets I will never share with anyone.

63. My secrets could get me in trouble.

64. I have secrets that would make some people think I'm crazy.

65. I've never told the truth about what somebody did to me.

66. I used to hate for certain people to give me a bath or shower.

67. There's a particular person who gives me a weird feeling.

68. Things have been done to me that I can never tell about.

69. I share a secret with a particular person.

70. Something bad happened to me that is my fault.

71. Something inside me caused another person to do something bad.

72. If I ever told the truth about what happened to me, someone would get in trouble.

73. If I ever told the truth about what happened to me, a person or a pet might be badly harmed.

74. The person I share a secret with is an adult.

75. The person I share a secret with is a child or teenager.

76. I keep thinking about my private parts.

77. I feel very hopeless about my situation.

Child Abuse Questions

36 - 45
47, 50, 56, 57, 60, 62, 63, 65,
66 – 77

Potential Aggression

1 – 35, 48 – 55, 58, 61, 63, 64, 68, 77

Examiner comments:

_____

_____

_____

_____

_____

_____

_____

_____

_____

If possible, Dr. Ewart would appreciate an anonymous copy for the test data bank.

Dr. H.B. Ewart, 131 S. Wise Drive, Sumter, SC 29150

Substance Abuse Test for Resistant Students or Employees

When seeking to predict the possibility of violence, whether school or workplace, it can also be important to check for substance abuse. Such is the case where an employee or student has resisted positive change. This test is designed for those who have been uncooperative when other means of intervention has already been tried.

Interviewer: Insist on eye contact with each response. Mark "T" (true) or "U" (untrue) beside each question according to your personal impression.

1. Are you ever afraid that someone might think you are under the influence of drugs?
2. Do your social activities involve any type of drug use?
3. Do you ever get away from other people in order to take a drug?
4. Do you stay away from social events when drugs won't be included?
5. Do you ever take more of a prescription medicine than what is ordered?
6. Do you ever use illegal drugs on top of prescription medicines?
7. What prescription drugs do you take?
8. What is the strength of your prescription medicine, and how often do you take it?
9. Has anyone ever said you're acting strangely?
10. Does anyone suspect that you are on drugs?
11. Do you have a high tolerance for prescription medicines such as pain killers or tranquilizers? In other words, can you take a heavier dose than most people?
12. Do you use medicines to cope with stress?
13. Did you ever experiment with crack cocaine?
14. In the past year, have you changed friends or moved to a new location?
15. Do you ever feel guilty about using medicines or drugs?

16. Have you ever broken the law while under the influence of medicine or drugs?

17. Do you feel strongly that drugs should be legalized?

18. Do you have any medical condition that requires medication?

19. If the last question is "yes," do you follow the doctor's instructions?

20. Have you ever been late for work or missed work due to medicines or drugs?

21. How many of your friends are drug users?

22. Are you worried about a close friend's drug use?

23. Have you had major problems with employment due to drugs?

24. Do you live at a fairly low standard?

25. Do you rely on family or close friends for housing, food, or money?

26. Have you ever had an accident that occurred while you were using?

27. Are any of your important relationships in danger of ending?

28. Do you resent authority?

29. Do you ever feel angry or defensive?

30. Do you get angry when someone asks about your drug use?

31. Do you often pay your bills late?

32. Do you come up short on money before the next pay day?

33. Do you have any disabilities that are difficult to cope with?

34. Is your stress in life greater than most people's?

15	# Workplace Violence	

Much workplace violence is sparked by stalkers who come to the workplace of their victims and harass or punish them on the job. Offices, factories, assembly plants, and even schools are at risk of an intruder stopping at nothing to get to his victim. As domestic violence increases, so does workplace violence. A great deal of abuse also arises from a superior to an employee, or even from a colleague nominally on the same level. This can even amount to physical torture, but is more often verbal, including the use of "humor", the issuing of arbitrary orders, isolation, malicious gossip, etc. Violence is not always physical. Therefore, it is wise for an employer to screen his female candidates for child and domestic abuse, with the tests earlier included. The screening that follows is particularly for men but may also reveal vital traits in female applicants. In addition, it is recommended that employers administer the "Substance Abuse Screen for Resistant Drug Abusers" on p. 155.

Test for Potentially Dangerous Employees

This questionnaire requires an experienced interviewer willing to call upon professional consultation before taking any definitive action.

To be asked out-loud by interviewer; response: "yes" or "no".

1. Sometimes it seems that my thoughts are broadcast so that others can hear them.

2. Others can read my thoughts.

3. I've heard voices that no one else could hear.

4. There are people who try to control my thoughts.

5. I'm the target of a conspiracy.

6. I've made plans about how to kill myself.

7. When I'm upset, I typically do something to hurt myself.

8. I have no interest in life.

9. Death would be a relief.

10. I'm considering suicide.

11. People are afraid of my temper.

12. Sometimes my temper explodes and I completely lose control.

13. Sometimes I'm very violent.

14. I've threatened to hurt people.

(Source of above items: *Personality Assessment Inventory*, Leslie Morey, Ph.D., Psychological Assessment Resources, Inc.)

15. I hope that I can retire early.

16. I only work because I have to.

17. People have wondered why I've had so many different jobs.

18. When I'm not employed, I sleep very late.

19. I'm really a night person, not a morning person.

20. I work better when left alone to do the job my own way.

21. I believe that drugs should be legalized.

22. I see nothing wrong with having a beer at lunch.

23. I'm not the kind of person who likes to join groups.

24. There is someone in my life who thinks he (or she) owns me.

25. I never have more than one or two very close friends.

26. I've broken off close relationships and then formed an intense friendship with somebody else.

27. Sometimes my mind drifts off into space, like I'm not here anymore.

28. I jump at sudden noises.

29. I have nightmares or flashbacks about past events.

30. Sometimes I think there's something wrong with my nerves.

31. I was abused as a child.

32. Fairly often, I have to ask people to repeat what they just told me.

33. People often make me repeat or explain what I've just said.

34. I think it's stupid that drugs haven't been legalized.

35. In my job history, I haven't been fired; I just quit.

36. If there was a company picnic, I probably wouldn't come.

37. I don't like doing the same job over and over again.

38. I get a lot of aches and pains when I work a long time.

39. Companies don't give enough rest breaks.

40. The supervisors I've worked for have been conceited; they think they're better than the workers.

Questions for multi-word response:

41. The real reason I left my last job is because
_____

42. The ideal type of job for me would be
_____

43. The main things I don't like about other people are _____

44. These are some of the things my other supervisors did wrong _____

45. The things that are wrong with this country are
_____

46. The reason I haven't lasted very long at jobs before is _____

47. The pay and benefits for this particular job should be _____

48. When I get home, here's how I spend my time
_____

49. The people I admire most in this world are
_____ and the reasons are
_____

50. The things I believe would make me a better worker are _____

51. My long-term goals in life are _____

###

Interviewer's impressions

_____

_____

_____

_____

_____

_____

_____

_____

_____

_____

_____

_____

_____

_____

Consultation indicated ____yes ____no

16 | The Falsely Accused

Victims in the Truest Sense

Falsely accused parents, usually fathers, are a rapidly growing population. The National Center for Child Abuse and Neglect reports 3.5 million cases of *alleged* child abuse in 1998, with 1 million of these *confirmed*. But 71 percent of the accusations were unfounded and *false*. (Tong, 2002).

One can only imagine the horror that a man like "David" in Chapter 10 (page 107) goes through when a child he dearly loves betrays him. Not only does he have a losing battle with a twisted court system rubber-stamping the zealous actions of the child-protective-service agency, he can never prove his innocence to the most important people in his life. Never knowing what his friends and family really think is the worst part of all.

The process goes on endlessly. Not only does the threat of jail hang over his head, but his family is destroyed. The child inventing the lies, usually in collusion with the mother, becomes only a pawn—also a victim, a weapon against a hated husband.

A great proportion of the false allegations are created by runaway teens, especially when they are running from juvenile court rather than from the father. When finally picked up by the police, they claim they ran away because they were being sexually abused by their father. Their accounts are not only detailed but disgusting, extremely graphic, and very well rehearsed, with the help of other runaways.

In most cases the teen has been further coached by Mother, who has her own stake in the outcome; that is, custody plus the cruelest possible punishment of the father. Often the child, the mother, or both are sociopathic liars hell-bent on getting their way.

The biggest problem is that there is rarely any evidence to disprove. So what defense does the falsely accused have?

Dean Tong, author of *Elusive Innocence: Survival Guide for the Falsely Accused,* is one of the nation's best experts on how a man can win his case. When writing this book, he asked me to contribute an appendix of questions that a defense attorney can ask during a deposition of the accusing child.

These interrogatories are so thorough and strong that I truly doubt that any lying teen could stand up against them. I urge most strongly that any defendant, if innocent, insist—and I mean *demand*—that his attorney ask the child *every single question.* Most of them are listed below. The full set is included as Appendix I in Tong's book.

Defense Interrogatories for False Accusers

1. Name all persons who have prepared you to answer questions during this session.

2. Before you ran away, did you have any intention of "getting even" with your father if he reported your absence to the police?

3. Did you disclose your plans to make up a story about your father to any of your friends?

4. How many interviewing sessions took place that dealt with accusations against your father?

5. Who conducted these interviews?

6. Did you take any tests?

7. How long did each interview last?

8. Did you take an oath to tell the truth when you were interviewed?

9. Who witnessed this oath?

10. Was a family history obtained from your mother?

11. Have you ever been sexually active with any boy or girl?

12. At what age was your first sexual experience with a boy or girl?

13. Were you ever reluctant about accusing your father?

14. Is there any benefit to you if you stick to your accusation?

15. When you made these accusations against your father, were you angry at him for other reasons?

16. If you were angry at him, why?

17. Were you angry at your mother?

18. Why were you angry at your mother?

19. When your mother took you to stay with your father, did you feel this was punishment or rejection? (Some mothers will purposely place the child in the father's care to provide a time-frame for alleged abuse.)

20. Why did you wait until your final runaway before accusing your father? Why not the first time you ran away?

21. Why did you not tell your therapist or your school counselor that your father molested you?

22. Why did you not tell your pastor or any other family member?

23. If your father really molested you, why didn't you warn your brother(s) and sister(s)?

24. What reasons can you think of that your father would take you to a counselor and a priest, and encouraged you to stay with family members and friends when you could tell any one of them that he molested you?

25. Describe in detail your memory of your father molesting you. Include the place and room, what you were wearing, what you were doing right before, what time of day it was, what he said, what you said, where he touched you and for how long, whether there was pain, how you felt, whether there was discharge or blood, whether you cried, whether you begged him to stop, and any other details that you remember. I will repeat each of these one at a time and give you time to think before you answer.

26. Please describe your most horrible memory of being abused?

27. Do you suffer from flashbacks (explain), night sweats, or nightmares due to the abuse?

28. What do you see in your nightmares and flashbacks, and how do you feel?

29. If you told your counselor other things before you ran away, why didn't you mention the abuse?

30. Have you even made any complaints to anyone about these matters, and what did you say?

31. Do you have any friends who have made similar accusations about a parent?

32. Please name other people you have had sex with, and whether they were children, teens, or adults.

33. Do you understand that any adult who had sex with you, or sheltered you while considered a runaway will be prosecuted as a criminal?

34. You were willing to accuse your father. Are you willing to name anybody in the last question? I'll repeat it.

35. Was anyone who sheltered you a drug dealer? Anyone into "kiddie porn"?

36. Where can we find the people in the last question?

37. Do you know that lying in an interview like this one, under oath, is a crime in itself?

38. Has anyone told you what perjury is and what the penalty is?

39. Do you think your mother will benefit if your father is punished?

40. When you were still a runaway, whom did you tell about your father? How can we reach this person or these people?

41. Can you contact the people you were with during your runaway and ask them to come in?

42. If you know, please name the classification that your accusation was placed in. I'll explain each as I name them. They are:

- Credible disclosure—suspicion of abuse supported.

- Credible non-disclosure—no or low index of suspicion remains.

- Non-credible disclosure—evidence of coaching or other factors decreases or   removes suspicion of abuse.

- Unclear—high index of suspicion remains, but no disclosure or problematic disclosure exists.

43. Do you feel your mother has added credibility to your accusations against your father, and if so, how?

44. What kinds of accusations has your mother made about your father to other members of the family?

45. What have you purposely not told me?

References

Alexander, R.C. and Durfee, D.T. *Perspective of the U.S. Advisory Board on Child Abuse and Neglect,* "The APSAC Advisor, Special Issue on Child Fatalities," 7, 4 (1994)

American Psychiatric Association. *Diagnostic Criteria from DSM-IV.* Washington, D.C. (1994)

Ames, Louis B. "Child Psychology," *in Grolier's Encyclopedia* (1993)

Baumrind, D. *Parenting Styles and Adolescent Development.* In Lerner, R.M., Peterson, A.C., and Brooks-Gunn, J. (eds.) *Encyclopedia of Adolescence.* New York: Garland (1991)

Bechler, R.F. and Hudson, L. Developmental Psychology: An Introduction (1986)

Briere, J., Evans, D., Runtz, M. & Wall, T. *Symptomatology* in *Men Who Were Molested as Children: A Comparison Study.* "American Journal of Orthopsychiatry," *58* (1988)

Castallo, M. and Ewart, H. *A Carnation a Day.* Philadelphia: Dorrance & Company, (1977)

Cerny, J. in *Human Development Guide.* http://pulua.hcc.hawaii.edu (1996)

Disciplining Children in America: A Gallup Poll Report, December, 1995

Egeland, B. Stroufe, L.A., and Erickson, M.F. *Developmental Consequences of Different Patterns of Maltreatment.* "Child Abuse and Neglect, 7 (1983)

Erickson, M. and Egeland, B. Throwing a Spotlight on the Developmental Outcomes for Children: Findings of a Seventeen-Year Follow-Up Study. Internet Trauma and Abuse Domain (1996).

Finkelhor, D. *A Sourcebook on Child Sexual Abuse.* Beverly Hills: Sage Publications (1989)

Frankl, V. *Man's Search for Meaning.* Washington, D.C.: Washington Square Press (1998)

FreudNet: Internet Reference Page (1996)

Fromuth, M.E. & Burkhart, B.R. Long-Term Psychological Correlates of Childhood Sexual Abuse in Two Samples of College Men. "Child Abuse and Neglect", 13 (1989)

Grohol, A. *Child Sexual Abuse.* Mental Health Domain, Internet (1996)

Heise, L. Ending Violence Against Women. Associated Press (1999)

Herman, J. *Trauma and Recovery.* New York: Basic Books (1992)

Hopper, J. *Sexual Abuse Prevalence Studies.* hopper@cybercom.net (1996)

Hotchin, S. Abuse Against Women a Health Issue. Baltimore: Associated Press (2000)

Hotchin, S. *Study: Third of All Women Abused.* Baltimore: Associated Press (2000)

Hunter, J.A. A Comparison of the Psychosocial Adjustment of Adult Males and Females Sexually Molested as Children. "Journal of Interpersonal Violence," 6 (1991)

Huyer, D. Thoracoabdominal Trauma in Child Abuse. "Perspective of the U.S. Advisory Board on Child Abuse and Neglect,"The APSAC Advisor, Special Issue on Child Fatalities, 7, 4 (1994)

Kaplan, Bernard, "Developmental Psychology," in *Grolier's Encyclopedia* (1993)

Kotler, J.A. and Brown, R.W. *Introduction to Therapeutic Counseling* (2nd Ed.) Pacific Grove: Brooks/Cole (1992)

Lehman, B. *A Catalogue of Mennonite and Amish Resources.* Denver: Mennonite Foundation (1996)

Levinson, D.J. *A Concept of Adult Development.* "American Psychologist," 41 (1986)

Lew, M. *Victims No Longer.* New York: Nevraumont (1992)

Lisak, D. The Psychological Impact of Sexual Abuse: Content Analysis of Interview with Male Survivors. "Journal of Traumatic Stress," 7 (1994)

Myers, M.D. *Men Sexually Assaulted as Adults and Sexually Abused as Boys.* 13th Annual Canadian Sex Research Forum Conference. "Archives of Sexual Behavior," 18 (1989)

Nelson, B. Internet Domain, Psychology, Abuse Pages (1996)

Olson, P.E. The Sexual Abuse of Boys: A Study of the Long-Term Psychological Effects. In Hunter, M. (Ed.) The Sexually Abused Male: Vol 1. *Prevalence, Impact and Treatment.* Lexington, MA: Lexington Books (1990)

Peck, M. S. *People of the Lie, The Hope for Healing Human Evil._New York: Touchstone, Simon & Schuster (1983)

Piaget, J. *The Moral Development of the Child* (1932; repr. 1965)

Rothbart, M.K. Temperament and the Development of Inhibited Approach. *Child Development,* 59 (1988

Shakeshaft, C. *Sexual Abuse of Student by School Personnel.* "Phi Delta Kappan," 514 (March, 1995)

Shulman, T.E. *Child Abuse in Schools: Under Investigation.* ENWR 101, Section 8 (Fall, 1995)

Smith, W.L. *Abusive Head Injury.* "Perspective of the U.S. Advisory Board on Child Abuse and Neglect,"*The APSAC Advisor,* 7, 4 (1994)

Special Issue on Child Fatalities, The APSAC Advisor. Chicago: American Professional Society on the Abuse of Children, (1994)

Tong, D. *Elusive Innocence. Survival Guide for the Falsely Accused.* Lafayette, LA: Huntington House Publishers (2005)

U.S. Department of Health and Human Services, *Child Maltreatment 1995: Reports from the States to the National Child Abuse and Neglect Data System.*

Washington, D.C.: U.S. Government Printing Office (1997)

U.S. Department of Health and Human Services, *The Third National Incidence Study of Child Abuse and Neglect.* Washington, D.C.: U.S. Government Printing Office (1996)

U.S. Department of Justice, *Wives Are the Most Frequent Victims in Family Murders.* Press Release (July 10, 1994)

Walker, A.G. *Cognitive Interviewing, 2* (July/August, 1995)

Walker, A.G. *Handbook on Questioning Children: A Linguistic Perspective.* Washington, D.C.: ABA Center on Children and the Law (1994)

World Headquarters, Alcoholics Anonymous, New York, NY, Telephone interview (March, 1999)

About the Author

Fr. Heyward B. Ewart, III, Ph.D. has devoted more than 24 years of his professional life to the protection and treatment of women, children, and the family. During the Carter administration, he served the White House Conference on Families, and such leadership continues to this day. He is not only a veteran clinician in the mental health field, but also a distinguished teacher at the university level and an active chaplain. Through Zoe University in Jacksonville, Florida, his video lectures have been used by distance-learning students across the United States and in some 41 foreign countries.

A Diplomate of the American College of Forensic Examiners, he has served as an expert trial witness in several states. He has also conducted continuing education at the University of North Florida and University Hospital of Jacksonville, FL.

A much sought-after public speaker, Dr. Ewart is a commanding presenter who speaks with great passion on the issues of abused women and children. He has hosted and appeared as a guest on many TV and radio programs in major markets, a love that dates back to his original career as a radio and TV news announcer.

He is a published poet, and his hobbies also include photography, singing, drama, and social activities of all kinds.

http://www.child-to-adult-victim.com

Index

9 781932 690330